A Biblical Explanation for Evil

By Troy J. Edwards

Unless otherwise indicated, all Scripture quotations are taken from the *King James Version* (KJV) of the Bible.

WHY?

A Biblical Explanation for Evil

Troy J. Edwards

Copyright © 2015 by Troy J. Edwards

Cover design by the artistically creative team of Teri Mayumi Edwards and Takako Edwards

Published by **Vindicating God Ministries**

The author gives permission to have any portion of this book copied if it will assist other believers in receiving all that God has for them and/or if it will lead someone to Christ. The material here is for the edification of the body of Christ. However, it is a violation of Christian ethics to use the author's material for personal profit gain. Remember that we must all stand before the judgment seat of Christ to give an account for the deeds that are done in the body (1 Cor. 3:8-15). Therefore, please comply within the limits of this permission statement.

Contents

Preface	5
1. Why Does Evil Exist if God is Good?	7
2. Why Did One Sin Cause all of This?	19
3. Why the Forbidden Tree in the Garden?	31
4. Why Didn't God Destroy Satan? (Part One)	43
5. Why Didn't God Destroy Satan? (Part Two)	55
6. Why Does the Bible Attribute Evil to God?	65
7. Why is Satan Absent in the Old Testament?	77
8. Why Did God Create if He Knew?	89
9. Why Doesn't God Intervene and Stop Evil?	101
10. Why So Much Warfare and Bloodshed?	111
11. Why Did Jesus have to Die for Our Sins?	123
12. Why Must Sinners Suffer in Hell?	135
13. Why are Christians Confused about Evil?	147
14. Why is God Waiting so Long to Destroy Evil?	159
Notes	171
Other Books by Troy J. Edwards	175

Dedicated to the loving memory of my big sister

Julia Ann Edwards

What happened to you was not fair. Neither was it God. It was evil at work.

Preface

In this book I want to prove to the reader that the Bible offers a satisfactory answer to the "why" questions many have in relation to an omnipotent but good God in contrast to the rampant heart-breaking evil we see in our world.

Many scholars and philosophers with much higher education and greater intellectual acumen than I possess have attempted to provide answers to the nature of evil in our world while defending God's goodness and justice. I have spent years searching and reading material on this subject. I have found some that was helpful and much that wasn't.

To be honest, many people are fed up with the standard Christian responses on this subject. Though some claim to give *Biblical* answers to our "why" questions we often receive responses that consign much of God's alleged activity to "divine mysterious purposes." This is a subtle indication that the Bible, containing 66 books full of information about God and His ways, has no definitive answer to our "why" questions about evil.

I have never been able to accept that. Since God took the time to have His Word communicated to us in the form of the Bible then it seems prudent that He would want us to understand why this world is in the terrible shape that it is in. He would also want to answer those questions as to why He supposedly let this happen and why He has not seemingly done anything about it as of yet.

I also believe that God would want us to get past much of the convoluted philosophy that has crept into the church via our theologians and understand the truth about His omnipotence and sovereignty as it relates to evil. I believe that He would want this done in a way that is not only Biblical but makes sense. To hold contrasting views about God that claim that He is good and not the author of evil but then say that He secretly willed all of this because He is omnipotent and sovereign does not make sense. Neither is it "spiritual." It is only convoluted unbiblical philosophy consigned to the realm of mystery because its advocates realize that such foolishness cannot be explained.

In this book it is my desire that my nearly 30 years of searching the Bible and other material for answers to the types of questions addressed in this book will finally provide a Biblical understanding of this subject. I pray that I will be able to answer some of *your* "why" questions in a satisfactory manner. I don't claim to have *all* of the answers and I know that some answers might generate more questions. But I believe that the answers I provide here are enough to vindicate God's goodness and justice in the light of evil.

Most of all, I hope that this book will help you to see a picture of a loving God who never planned any of this evil and pain. I hope you will see that He is at war with evil, is doing all that He can to rescue us from evil now and who will, in His omnipotence, one day rid this universe of evil forever. I want you to fall in love with this God. His Name is Yahweh (Father, Son, and Holy Spirit). Three persons but One God!

Chapter One

Why Does Evil Exist if God is Good?

We know that whoever is born of God does not sin; but he who has been born of God keeps himself, and the wicked one does not touch him. We know that we are of God, and **the whole world lies under the sway of the wicked one** (1 John 5:18-19; New King James Version)

The Bible describes Satan, the devil, as the "wicked one" (Mat. 13:19, 38; Eph. 6:16; 1 John 2:13, 14; 3:12; 5:18, 19) and "the evil one" (Mat. 5:37; 6:13; John 17:15; 2 Thess. 3:3). One translation of verse 19 says, *"....the whole world is under the control of the evil one"* (God's Word). Another translation says, *"....the whole world belongs to the devil"* (World English New Testament). The Living Bible paraphrases it, *"....all the rest of the world around us is under Satan's power and control."* Satan is the god and present ruler of this evil world (Luke 4:5-6; John 12:31; 14:30; 16:11; Eph. 2:2; 6:10-12; 2 Cor. 4:4; Gal. 1:4).

The *short* answer to the question being asked in this chapter is that evil exists though God is good because the world is presently under the control of the evil one. This goes against the popular notion that "God is in control." During the millennial reign of Christ Satan will be bound for a thousand years. God will then "be in control" and people will see that God's reign is one in which nothing shall *"hurt nor destroy in all my holy mountain."* (Isa. 11:1-10; 65:17-29; Rev. 20:1-6). When this happens we will see that God was never responsible for the evil conditions of this world.

The Mystery of Evil Revealed
Within Christian academic circles there is a theological discipline referred to as "theodicy". This is the attempt to answer the ages old question as to why there is evil in this world if the God who created this world is good, kind, and powerful. This is often referred to as the "problem" (or "mystery") of evil.

Many theologians have attempted to solve the problem of evil by either making God the direct cause of it or teaching that He preordained that evil would take place as a part of His sovereign plan. The fact that a good God would ordain evil for a divine purpose leaves many perplexed. Therefore His reasons are consigned by theologians to the realm of *mystery*.

Theologians and philosophers also attempt to explain the origin and "mystery" of evil while making little or no mention of Satan. This is a major mistake. It has led to making God the responsible agent for evil by so-called "best world" and "greater good" philosophies.

If we would stop looking to God as the source or responsible agent for evil then the "mystery" disappears. Theologians and philosophers have spent centuries wrestling with this "mystery", but God has already revealed it to us:

> *And now ye know what withholdeth that he might be revealed in his time.* ***For the mystery of iniquity doth already work:*** *only he who now letteth will let, until he be taken out of the way. And then shall that Wicked be revealed, whom the Lord shall consume with the spirit of his mouth, and shall destroy with the brightness of his coming: Even him, whose coming is after the working of* ***Satan with all power and***

> ***signs and lying wonders***, *And with all deceivableness of unrighteousness in them that perish; because they received not the love of the truth, that they might be saved.* (2 Thess. 2:6-10)

Another translation says, *"For the secret of evil is even now at work: but there is one who is keeping back the evil till he is taken out of the way"* (2 Thess. 2:7; Bible in Basic English). There is no need to wrestle with "mysteries" when God has placed the answer within our grasp. The Bible connects the "mystery" of evil to Satan, thus taking away the so called "problem" and "mystery". God desires that everyone, especially His own people, have knowledge of all so-called mysteries (Mark 4:11; Rom. 11:25; 16:25; 1 Cor. 2:7-10; Eph. 1:9; 6:19; Col. 4:3). This includes the so-called "mystery of evil".

    God is not ordaining evil but is the One restraining, or rather, holding back the full consequences of it. The day will come when God will loosen the restraints and allow Satan and evil to have full reign. In the meantime the so-called "mystery" concerning evil has been revealed to the Christian. God has nothing to do with it. He is at war with it. Satan is the one behind evil.

    Some wonder why an all-powerful God cannot stop evil. 2 Thess. 2:6-10 tells us that God, in His love and mercy, is restraining the full consequences of the evil that *man* invites into this world, demonstrating that He is certainly more powerful than the evil one. Through great power and tender mercy He does not presently allow the full consequences of evil. He cannot stop all evil because man, to whom God gave an irrevocable dominion over the earth, continually invites in evil through his sin and rebellion (Gen. 1:26-28; Psalm 8:6. See also Rom. 5:12; 1 Cor. 15:21; Luke 4:6). At present, God must allow man the free choice to either submit to Him or continue to yield to Satan (Gen. 4:7; 1 John 3:8-12; Eph. 4:27; James 4:7; 1 Pet. 5:8-9).

How Did Satan become Evil?
The longer explanation as to why evil exists despite the fact that God is infinitely good begins with the *origin* of evil itself. Evil never began with the Triune God. First of all, the Triune God (Father, Son, and Holy Spirit) has no beginning. He has always been and always shall be as far as *existence* is concerned. Furthermore, He has been and always shall be exceedingly good as far as *character* is concerned (Psalm 25:8; 34:8; 86:5; 106:1; 107:1; 118:1, 29; 119:68; 135:3; 136:1; Mat. 19:17).

Only goodness is eternal and only goodness has always been in existence. Goodness has no starting point. Goodness has always been because God has always been. Evil, on the other hand, has a beginning and will, thank God, have an ending. Since evil has a beginning then it has to have begun with a *finite* creature and not with an *infinite* Creator. That finite creature is known today as "the devil" and "Satan" (Rev. 12:9-11). In Genesis 1:1-2 we read the following:

> *In the beginning, God created the heavens and the earth. Now, the earth,* **had become waste and wild**, *and darkness, was on the face of the roaring deep,—but, the Spirit of God, was brooding on the face of the waters* (Rotherham Emphasized Bible - Emphasis are mine)

The Concordant Literal Translation renders verse 2, *"Yet the earth* **became a chaos and vacant***, and darkness was on the surface of the submerged chaos."* In order to understand the origin of evil we need to understand that there is a large gap of time, perhaps millions, maybe even billions of years between Genesis 1 verses 1 and 2. In verse 1 God created. Verse 2 is *not* a description of the original creation:

> *For thus says Yahweh, Creator of the heavens; He is the Elohim, and Former of the earth, and its Maker, and He, He established it.* ***He did not create it a chaos****. He formed it to be indwelt. "I am Yahweh, and there is none else."* (Isa. 45:18; Concordant Literal Translation)

The VOICE translation says, *"He didn't make it a disorganized wasteland but made it a beautiful and comfortable home."* Something happened between verses 1 and 2 that is totally contrary to God's purposes. It was during the lengthy period of time between these two verses that Satan sinned and fell which resulted in chaos.

In the beginning God created a universe free of evil. When God created the universe evil was never contemplated. There was no flaw or evil in God's creation (Eccl. 3:11). It was sheer absolute perfection. There was no war, sickness, or poverty. There were no trials or problems. There was no such thing as temptation and sin. There was nothing but happiness and harmony throughout creation. It was a universe fueled by unselfish, others-focused, *agape* love. God is love (1 John 4:16). Everything He does, to include creating, is done from the basis of unselfish love.

God Did not Create the Devil

Jesus is the creator of all that is (John 1:1-4). Numerous *good* angels were a part of His creation:

> *For by him were all things created, that are in heaven, and that are in earth, visible*

> *and invisible, whether they be thrones, or dominions, or principalities, or powers: all things were created by him, and for him: And he is before all things, and by him all things consist.* (Col. 1:16-17)

> *And the angel which I saw stand upon the sea and upon the earth lifted up his hand to heaven, And sware by him that liveth for ever and ever,* **who created heaven, and the things that therein are***, and the earth, and the things that therein are, and the sea, and the things which are therein, that there should be time no longer* (Rev. 10:5-6)

Jesus is the creator of the angelic beings; the *Seraphim* (Isa. 6:1-3), the *Cherubim* (Ezek. 1:5-10), and a numerous host of other angels (Heb. 12:22). There were at least three *archangels* (chief, ruling or leading angel). Michael (Rev. 12:7), Gabriel (Dan. 8:16-19; Luke 1:19-26), and an anointed cherub named *Lucifer* (*Morning-star*). Lucifer would later become known as *Satan* (Luke 14:12).

However, while most of the angels would remain loyal to God, Lucifer, with other angels following him, turned against the Lord and waged war on his kingdom:

> *And there was war in heaven: Michael and his angels fought against the dragon; and the dragon fought and his angels, And prevailed not; neither was their place found any more in heaven. And the great dragon was cast out, that old serpent, called the Devil, and Satan, which deceiveth the whole world: he was cast out*

into the earth, and his angels were cast out with him. (Rev. 12:7-9)

Though a future war, like most Bible prophecy, Rev. 12:7-9 also glimpses the past. Lucifer and a third of the angels (Rev. 12:3-4) rebelled and war ensued. However, Satan ("accuser" and "adversary"), the devil ("slanderer") did not begin this way. God created a perfect angel who later *became* a devil of his own volition. Origen (182-254 AD), refuting an anti-Christian philosopher named Celsus, wrote:

> "I have not yet mentioned the passages in Ezekiel, where he speaks, as it were, of Pharaoh, or Nebuchadnezzar, or the prince of Tyre; or those in Isaiah, where lament is made for the king of Babylon, **from which not a little might be learned concerning evil, as to the nature of its origin and generation**, and as to how it derived its existence from some who had lost their wings, and who had followed him who was the first to lose his own"[1] (emphasis mine)

God is not at all responsible for the being we now know as "Satan" and "the devil". He is not responsible for the numerous fallen angels and demons that work with Satan to bring evil into the universe. The origin of evil does not begin with God, but with Satan's free-will act of rebellion *against* God.

Evil is the Violation of God's Love

God's commandment to His angels was simply to love Him and one another (Mark 12:31; John 13:34; 14:21; 15:10, 17; 1 John 3:23; 4:21; 5:2-3; 2 John 1:5-6). We know this to be a commandment to angels because God is love (1 John 4:7-8).

From the beginning of his creation Lucifer (Light bearer) fully adhered to God's commandment of love. But one day Lucifer began to become self–centered and proud. He began to have new ambitions that were in contrast to God's love command. Lucifer's "will" became opposed to God's will:

> *How art thou fallen from heaven, O Lucifer, son of the morning! how art thou cut down to the ground, which didst weaken the nations! For thou hast said in thine heart, **I will** ascend into heaven, **I will** exalt my throne above the stars of God: **I will** sit also upon the mount of the congregation, in the sides of the north: **I will** ascend above the heights of the clouds; **I will** be like the most High. Yet thou shalt be brought down to hell, to the sides of the pit* (Isa. 14:12-15)

Part of Lucifer's new ambitions was to exalt his throne above the "stars". Stars in this context are a reference to the other angels (Judges 5:20; Job 38:7; Rev. 1:20; 12:1-4). Lucifer wanted to exalt himself above the angels. He wanted to take charge and become a tyrant and dictator. Lucifer's "I wills" reveal how he became selfish and self-focused, concerned only with what *he* wanted. The basis of sin is caring only for oneself.

Evil was introduced when God's love command was opposed by the self-seeking will of another. Before this, God's created universe had no evil. It was a place of love, joy, contentment, fulfilment, excitement, fun and safety. There was never anything to fear. This was because the angels obeyed God's Word of love.

In the universe, there was one will – the will of unselfish, others-focused love. Lucifer's selfish will went against the love-will of the Triune Godhead. When Lucifer opposed a will that is good then evil was born and he was the father of it (John 8:44). Clarence Larkin stated it well when he wrote:

> "As long as Satan chose the 'Will of God,' there was no 'Evil' in the universe, but the moment he chose to follow his own Will, then he fell, and by persuading others to follow him he introduced 'Evil' into the universe. The root of sin is SELFISHNESS..."[2]

God's kingdom and nature is pure, unadulterated, agape love. God's love nature does not seek its own (1 Cor. 13:4-7) but is "others-focused" rather than self-focused. It sacrifices for the good of others and is willing to give even at great loss to Himself (John 3:16; 15:13; Rom. 5:5-8; 1 John 4:7-11).

God's kingdom always ran <u>on the basis of love</u>. Satan introduced <u>selfishness</u> – ambition to be and have something in spite of the harm that it brings to others. This brought a contrast between his nature and that of God's (1 John 3:10-12). The basis of Satan's nature is murderous hatred (John 8:44). He stopped loving God and his fellow angels and followed blind selfish ambition. Satan rebelled against God's love.

Lucifer became a "Satan"

A vitally important truth about love is that, in order for it to be genuine, it must have the freedom to also *not* love. The Apostle Paul wrote, *"....use not liberty for an occasion to the flesh, but by love serve one another"* (Gal. 5:13). Love cannot be forced or coerced. One must be able to freely choose to love or not love.

God had given His angels freedom. In such a loving atmosphere there was never any reason to use this freedom to go against God's commandment to love. Furthermore, God had created an atmosphere in which every desire of the heart could be met as long as it did not violate the law of unselfish love. In Ezekiel 28 we see how God had created Lucifer with magnificent beauty and wisdom. God gave Lucifer multiple gifts and room for great achievements:

> *Son of man, take up a lamentation upon the king of Tyrus, and say unto him, Thus saith the Lord GOD; Thou sealest up the sum, full of wisdom, and **perfect in beauty.** Thou hast been in Eden the garden of God; every precious stone was thy covering, the sardius, topaz, and the diamond, the beryl, the onyx, and the jasper, the sapphire, the emerald, and the carbuncle, and gold: the workmanship of thy tabrets and of thy pipes was prepared in thee in the day that thou wast created.* (Ezek. 28:12-13)

God did not create an evil creature (Eccl. 3:11; Deut. 32:4). God created the one currently known as Satan with wisdom. God made him perfect in beauty. The anointed *cherub* currently known as Satan was created perfect and flawless. Iniquity was actually *found* in him later:

> *Thou art the anointed cherub that covereth; and I have set thee so: thou wast upon the holy mountain of God; thou hast walked up and down in the midst of the stones of fire.* ***Thou wast perfect in thy ways from the day that thou wast created, till iniquity was found in thee.*** (Ezek. 28:14-15)

God *discovered* iniquity in in Lucifer. The fact that God *found* iniquity in Lucifer means that He had nothing to do with the origin of evil. Therefore, G. H. Pember is correct when he says that this verse, "....shows that God is not the author of evil."[3] The origin of evil begins with Lucifer's opposition to God's unselfish love.

Most of the early church fathers believed that Ezekiel is dealing with Satan's downfall. The early church did not have the struggles with the so-called "problem" or "mystery" of evil that we have today.[4] Church Father Tertullian (160-225 AD) taught from Ezekiel 28 that God was in not responsible for Satan:

> If, however, you choose to transfer the account of evil from man to the devil as the instigator of sin, and in this way, too, throw the blame on the Creator, inasmuch as He created the devil—for He makes those spiritual beings, the angels— then it will follow that what was made, that is to say, the angel, will belong to Him who made it; while that which was not made by God, **even the devil, or accuser, cannot but have been made by itself**; and this by false detraction from God.... If you turn to the prophecy of Ezekiel, you will at once perceive that this angel was both by creation good and by choice corrupt.[5] (Emphasis are mine)

Therefore, evil was birthed into our universe by blind selfish hatred and selfish ambition through the archangel formerly known as Lucifer.

Pride was Satan's Ultimate Downfall

Paul taught the attributes of God's unselfish love when he wrote, *"Charity suffereth long, and is kind; charity envieth not;* **charity vaunteth not itself, is not puffed up***, Doth not behave itself unseemly, seeketh not her own, is not easily provoked, thinketh no evil"* (1 Cor. 13:4-5). This is the exact opposite direction taken by Lucifer. He became puffed up because of his beauty:

> ***Thine heart was <u>lifted up</u> because of thy beauty**, thou hast corrupted thy wisdom by reason of thy brightness: I will cast thee to the ground, I will lay thee before kings, that they may behold thee.* (Eze. 28:17)

Paul warns church leaders not to appoint new converts into church leadership when he writes, *"Not a novice, lest being **<u>lifted up</u>** with pride he fall into the condemnation of the devil"* (1 Tim. 3:6). The natural law of *cause and effect* brought the devil into condemnation and continues to do so with anyone who follows his example. Evil begins when love is absent. Love is unselfish and is not prideful. On the other hand, Jesus, who is God, took the very opposite route that Satan took by becoming a man to redeem man from Satan's reign (Phil. 2:5-8).[6] It is significant that Jesus chose to demonstrate that God Himself is willing to become a servant, proving that His way of ruling is completely different than Lucifer's (Matt. 23:8-12; Mark 10:41-45; John 13:1-15).

Since God is humble and evil begins with pride we conclude that the "mystery" of why evil came into being has nothing to do with God but with the self-absorbed, unloving prideful creature who began as good but later abused the freedom given to him by God. This was not a part of God's plan for the universe but the day is coming when God will surely rid it from His universe forever.

Chapter Two

Why Did One Sin Cause all of This?

Wherefore, as by one man sin entered into the world, and death by sin; and so death passed upon all men, for that all have sinned (Rom. 5:12)

There is no doubt that our world is currently a chaotic mess. Terrorists here and abroad are killing without compassion. Innocent children are being kidnapped, molested, and raped. Children who escape this particular horror are sometimes subject to parental abuse, starvation, drive-by shootings, and other evils. Crime continues to ravage neighborhoods and city streets. Corruption fills our corporations and our governments. The fear of sickness, disease, and financial deprivation haunt many on a daily basis. The list can go on.

What perplexes many Bible readers most is that all of this came about by *one sin*. All of the evil mentioned above came into the world by one single act of disobedience.

Warning or Threat?

Some period after Satan's fall and initial destruction of the earth, God began a six day restoration. It was during this period that He created man and gave him reign over the earth (Psalm 8:5-6; 115:16). God also commissioned man to use his delegated dominion to guard the earth against intruders. In Genesis 1 we read:

> *And God said, Let us make man in our image, after our likeness: and **let them have dominion** over the fish of the sea, and over the fowl of the air, and over the*

> *cattle, **and over all the earth**, and over every creeping thing that creepeth upon the earth. So God created man in his own image, in the image of God created he him; male and female created he them. And God blessed them, and God said unto them, be fruitful, and multiply, and replenish the earth, and **subdue it**: **and have dominion** over the fish of the sea, and over the fowl of the air, and over **every living thing** that moveth upon the earth."*
> (Gen. 1:26-28)

God blessed man and gave him dominion over creation. Man was to *subdue* the earth and *take dominion* over it. To "subdue" means to *"conquer"* and *"to bring into subjection."* This implies that there was already an enemy that Adam would have to deal with. However, having been given God's authority, which is naturally backed by God's power, Adam was more than ready to successfully deal with any enemy intruder.

However, Adam, like us today, could only exercise this authority while remaining submitted to God. James 4:7 says, *"Submit yourselves therefore to God. Resist the devil, and he will flee from you."* As long as Adam remained submitted to God then Satan could cause him no significant problems. God warned Adam about the negative effects that come with a failure to obey:

> *And the Lord God took the man, and put him into the garden of Eden to dress it and to keep it. And the Lord God commanded the man, saying, Of every tree of the garden thou mayest freely eat: But of the tree of the knowledge of good and evil, thou shalt not eat of it: for **in the day that***

thou eatest thereof thou shalt surely die (Gen. 2:15-17)

Note that God did not tell Adam, "If you eat from the tree of the knowledge of good and evil then I will kill you." God was not threatening Adam. He was warning Him about how His actions could cause severe damage, not only to himself, but all that he had been given dominion over. Rather than reading the passage as though God was *threatening* Adam, we need to instead see Him as *warning* Adam about the consequences that his disobedience would bring.

The Scripture tells us, *"Be ye angry, and **sin not**: let not the sun go down upon your wrath: Neither give place to the devil"* (Eph. 4:26-27). Our sin places us under satanic dominion (1 John 3:8-12). God was not threatening to kill Adam but warning him about how his disobedience would bring him under the government of Satan who rules through death (Rom. 5:17; Eph. 2:1-2; Heb. 2:14-15).

Adam Yielded to Death

Every Bible reader is well aware of the fact that that Adam did not heed God's warning. Satan came into the garden under the guise of a serpent (Gen. 3:1-5; Rev. 12:9; 20:2; 2 Cor. 11:3, 13-15). Satan falsely accused God to Eve of being an insecure, selfish liar. Satan suggested to Eve that God was holding back from her and Adam for selfish reasons. He brought doubts to her mind concerning God's love, goodness, and integrity. The sad result is that Adam and Eve accepted Satan's character assassination of God rather than to believe God's loving admonition. Even sadder is what happened afterwards:

> *And when the woman saw that the tree was good for food, and that it was pleasant to*

> *the eyes, and a tree to be desired to make one wise, she took of the fruit thereof, and did eat, and gave also unto her husband with her; and he did eat. And the eyes of them both were opened, and they knew that they were naked; and they sewed fig leaves together, and made themselves aprons. And they heard the voice of the LORD God walking in the garden in the cool of the day: and Adam and his wife **hid themselves from the presence of the LORD God** amongst the trees of the garden* (Gen. 3:6-8)

They disobeyed God by eating from the one tree God told them not to eat from. God had placed numerous fruit trees in the garden and gave them permission to freely eat from every single one of them except for that one particular tree. God gave them a great demonstration of His freedom and generosity but they allowed the devil to deceive them into believing that He was selfish, stingy, and trying to hold back from them.

As a result they *"hid themselves from the presence of the LORD God."* This is when Adam and Eve began to experience death. Those who are under the bondage of sin are said to be *"dead in trespasses and sins"* (Eph. 2:1b). God *is* life (Deut. 30:20; Psalm 36:9; John 11:25-26; 14:6; Acts 17:28; Gal. 2:20; Col. 3:3-4). Death is nothing more than separation from God who is the source of life:

> *But your iniquities have separated between you and your God, and your sins have hid his face from you, that he will not hear.* (Isa. 59:2)

> *"For whoso findeth me **findeth life**, and shall obtain favour of the Lord. But he that sinneth against me wrongeth his own soul: **all they that hate me love death**."* (Prov. 8:35,36)

> *"O Lord, the hope of Israel, all that forsake thee shall be ashamed, and they that depart from me shall be written in the earth, because they have forsaken the Lord, the fountain of living waters."* (Jer. 17:13; see also 2:13)

Many have been confused and some have even criticized the Bible because Adam and Eve supposedly did not *physically* die on the same day that they ate the fruit. This is a faulty understanding of the meaning of death. Death is not cessation of existence (annihilation), soul sleep, nor is it limited to separation of the spirit from the body. Death is *separation from the God*, the life-source! A literal rendering of Gen. 2:17 in the original Hebrew is "in dying you shall die," meaning separation from God will eventually lead to physical death.

Jesus prayed, *"And this is life eternal, that they might know thee the only true God, and Jesus Christ, whom thou hast sent"* (John 17:3). To know God is to have the life of God. Adam lost the eternal life he possessed when he stopped knowing and understanding God. He began to see God as unkind and capricious. Adam no longer valued God's Word to him. When we have placed ourselves under Satan's bondage of death then our understanding of God becomes twisted.

This caused a separation between Adam and God. Adam died spiritually that day because he separated himself from the protective life of God (Gen. 2:17; Isa. 59:1-2; Eph. 2:1-6), thus placing himself under Satan's kingdom of evil, darkness and death (Rom. 5:17; Col. 1:12-14; Heb. 2:14-15; 1 John 5:18-19). When we know God we will know Him as loving and not as someone "out to get us".

God is not a despot or a dictator. He gives men freedom to make choices for or against Him, but warns of the consequences of making the wrong choice.

> *See, I have set before thee this day life and good, and death and evil.... I call heaven and earth to record this day against you, that I have set before you life and death, blessing and cursing:* **therefore choose life**, *that both thou and thy seed may live* (Deut. 30:15, 19)

The tree represents the free choice that God had given to Adam. Adam had the choice of life or death. Nothing good was withheld from Adam. Even the Tree of Life was accessible to him. He was only forbidden from partaking of the one thing that would hurt him. In His love, God presents us with wonderful opportunities and nearly begs us to choose those against the alternatives which brings devastating consequences. Sadly, Adam chose separation from God, thereby choosing *death*.

Man Invites Satan to Rule through Death

Separation from God automatically placed man under Satan's government of death. Man was given the earth and dominion over it but chose to yield to Satan through sin:

> *Wherefore, as by one man sin entered into the world, and death by sin; and so death passed upon all men, for that all have sinned* (Rom. 5:12)

"Sin" and "evil" are synonymous (Gen. 50:17; 1 Kings 15:26, 34; 22:52; 2 Kings 13:2, 11; 14:24; 15:9, 18, 24, 28; 21:16). Furthermore "death" is synonymous with "evil" (Deut. 30:15). To plunge the world into sin and death is to plunge the world into evil. Why is there so much evil in the world? Adam chose to sin against God, thereby opening the door for Satan to bring his evil reign upon the earth.

Paul continues to write, *"For if by one man's offence **death reigned by one**"* (Rom. 5:17a) or as the Contemporary English Version puts it, *"Death ruled like a king because Adam had sinned."* When Adam and Eve disobeyed God, ate from the tree of the knowledge of good and evil and fell under a penalty of death, they, in essence, gave Satan reign of this world. The non-canonical book, **Wisdom of Solomon** says, "**Nevertheless through envy of the devil came death into the world**: and they that do hold of his side do find it" (2:23-24).

The Bible tells us that, *"He that committeth sin is of the devil"* (1 John 3:8). Peter adds, *"....for of whom a man is overcome, of the same is he brought in bondage"* (2 Pet. 2:19). When we sin we become a servant to sin (Rom. 6:16; John 8:34-35). Adam and Eve gave themselves over to Satan and thus died the moment they ate the fruit. They placed themselves and their descendants under Satan's government of death:

> *Forasmuch then as the children are partakers of flesh and blood, he also himself likewise took part of the same; that through death he might destroy him that had the power of death, that is, the devil; And deliver them who through fear of*

> *death were all their lifetime subject to bondage.* (Heb. 2:14-15)

Man was conquered by Satan and his government of death and *"through fear of death were **all their lifetime subject to bondage**".* By rebelling against God, Adam abdicated his God-given authority to Satan (Luke 4:5-8; John 12:31; 14:30; 16:11; Acts 26:18; 2 Cor. 4:4; Eph. 2:1-5; 6:10-12; Col. 1:13-14; 1 John 5:18-19). This is what Jesus came to recue us from.

This is why there is evil in the world today. Too often the so-called "mystery of why evil persists in this world" is wrongly centered on God's goodness. *Man* was given dominion over the earth and *man* allowed the devil to plunge this world and its habitants under a government of death. Most men have emulated the ways of Satan rather than God. Beginning with Adam and Eve, mankind under the influence of Satan, is selfish, caring only for themselves. The world's system, as controlled by Satan, has taught men to be this way. Therefore the majority of the world emulates the evil one. That is why there is so much evil in our world.

Satan's Legal Right to the Earth

Adam had been given full authority over the works of God's creation, but man sold out to the devil and sold us under his government of sin (Rom. 7:14). When man fell under Satan's tyranny, everything that God had placed in man's possession automatically became Satan's as well. In the temptation in the wilderness Satan tells Jesus:

> *And the devil, taking him up into an high mountain, shewed unto him all the kingdoms of the world in a moment of time. And the devil said unto him, All this power*

> *will I give thee, and the glory of them: for that is delivered unto me; and* **to whomsoever I will I give it** (Luke 4:5-6)

Jesus does not dispute any portion of Satan's claim here but simply defeats his temptation by the Word of God, thus making this particular temptation ineffective. Satan says, *"....to whomsoever I will I give it."* The father of lies was telling the basic truth here that whoever is in authority has a *legal* right to do with that which is given to him. The Psalmist said, *"....the earth hath he **given** to the children of men."* (Psalm 115:16b). Since the earth had been given to man, he had a legal right to give it away. That is exactly what man foolishly did.

While God has the physical power and might to wrest this world from Satan by force, this is not God's nature. God's omnipotent power is governed by His love, goodness, wisdom and His righteousness (2 Chron. 16:9; 1 Cor. 13:2; 14:1; 2 Cor. 6:7; 2 Thess. 1:11; Rev. 5:12; 7:12). When mankind sided with Satan he actually entered into a covenant with the kingdom of death (Isa. 28:15, 18). Sadly Satan had the *Covenant right* of ownership and God had to honor that.

Therefore, only a man who was not under death's authority could legally release mankind from the covenant (Rom. 5:15-21; 1 Cor. 15:21-22). If God acted in power outside of righteousness, thus violating His own righteous principles of covenant-keeping (Psalm 89:33-35), then Satan would have had legitimate accusations which would have placed doubts about God's character in the minds of His loyal angels and mankind itself.

The sin of Adam opened the door for Satan to rule and reign on the earth by covenant right. However, God has not so easily given up on man or left Him to remain under Satan's tyranny. There is something about the love of God that could not just forsake man after he took the devil's side. Therefore, God promised mankind a Savior that would help him to deal with his captor (Genesis 3:14-15). In Genesis God gave the very first prophecy about Jesus coming to earth as a man and His intentions to *legally* conquer Satan on our behalf.

The Principle of the Seed

All it took was one simple act of disobedience for Adam to abdicate his dominion and authority over the earth to the devil. This gave Satan full rights to bring all of the evil that we see and experience today. However, one still might rightfully ask, "How could Adam and Eve eating a piece of fruit bring so much major tragedy and catastrophe upon the world?"

When God created mankind He started with one man and woman who would partner with Him in propagating the whole race. Basically, Adam was the representative head for all of mankind: *"God began by making one man. From him came all the different people who live everywhere in the world"* (Acts 17:26; International Children's Bible). Adam's actions would determine the destiny for all of mankind. God put a lot of trust in Adam to have placed such a large responsibility upon him. God's idea was for the whole race to be blessed as the representative man overcame the one satanic obstacle, which was the forbidden tree. There was no reason for Adam to fail. Sadly, things went the exact opposite of God's intentions and, because of Adam, the whole race was plunged into disaster (Rom. 5:12, 18).

This is where we must come to understand "the principle of the seed." One small seed can produce a very large harvest. God established this principle within His creation (Gen. 1:11-12). This law was established by God only for good and not for evil (Prov. 3:9-10; Luke 6:37-38; 2 Cor. 9:6-8). Sadly, sin perverted the system and turned it into a system that works against us instead of for our benefit (Psalm 7:10-16; Prov. 1:24-33; 22:8-9; Jer. 4:18; Matt. 26:51-52; Gal. 6:7-9; James 1:14-15; Rom. 6:20-23).

The fact of the matter is that a small seed can produce a large harvest for good or for evil. The harvest from the seed is always much larger than the seed itself (Hosea 10:12-15). Therefore Adam's choice to disobey God became a small seed of sin that produced a great harvest of evil and devastation. Solomon well said:

> *For that they hated knowledge, and did not choose the fear of the LORD:* ***They would none of my counsel****: they despised all my reproof.* ***Therefore shall they eat of the fruit of their own way****, and be filled with their own devices* (Prov. 1:29-31)

The results of Adam's transgression showed immediately after he disobeyed God (Gen. 3:7). This *spiritual* death (that ultimately led to *physical* death) came upon Adam before God even showed up in the garden (Gen. 3:8-11). Therefore, this was not something that God personally inflicted upon Adam. Adam sowed the seeds of death when he rejected God's counsel, ate from the forbidden tree and produced a very large harvest as a result.

Satan Works through the "Seed" Principle

Satan has learned to work God's "seed" principle very well to accomplish his own nefarious ends. Jesus said:

> *The field is the world; the good seed are the children of the kingdom; but the tares are the children of the wicked one;* ***The enemy that sowed them is the devil****; the*

> *harvest is the end of the world; and the reapers are the angels* (Matt. 13:38-39)

Do we believe that God has created mosquitoes that suck blood and spread sickness? Do we believe that God created the parasites that kill? Do we believe that He created rats to spread diseases? Did God create scorpions that sting and kill? Did He create snakes to bite and give lethal injections to men and other animals?

It could very well be true that God created these animals and but He did not corrupt them with disease and death? The Bible tells us that Satan is the one who held the power of death (Heb. 2:14-15). That power was more than just symbolic. It had the ability to corrupt and distort God's good creation for evil purposes.

Death began to reign in the world due to sin (Rom. 5:12). This can only mean that before sin, scorpions did not sting people, rats did not spread disease, snakes did not bite and spread poison, and lions did not pounce and kill their prey. All of this violence is the result of the satanic distortion of God's wonderful creation.

Jesus' parable tells us that it is Satan, and not God, who is responsible for the bad among the good. God created everything good and Satan corrupted it. Satan has distorted God's creation and brought suffering upon it. The evil in creation is not God's work since He only gave us the "good seed."

Satan's use of God's seed system demonstrates how one act of sin can produce so great a harvest. A harvest comes with more seeds to plant and Satan utilizes these seeds to keep evil progressing in this world. This is a perversion of God's laws for sure, but it helps us once more to understand the "mystery" of evil.

Chapter Three

Why the Forbidden Tree in the Garden?

> *And the LORD God took the man, and put him into the garden of Eden to dress it and to <u>keep it</u>. And the LORD God commanded the man, saying, Of every tree of the garden thou mayest freely eat: But of the tree of the knowledge of good and evil, thou shalt not eat of it: for in the day that thou eatest thereof thou shalt surely die* (Gen. 2:15-17)

In the last chapter we pointed out the fact that God issued Adam a *warning* about the consequences of eating from the tree of the knowledge of good and evil. God was not *threatening* Adam because He had no intentions of hurting him one way or the other. But God did know of an enemy intruder who desired to hurt him, thus warning Adam to be on his guard.

Satan Present in the Garden
One of several reasons for embracing the gap between Genesis 1:1 and 2 is how it explains Satan's presence in the Garden of Eden and his malicious intent. All of the theories espoused by young earth creationists and others who scoff at the truth concerning the gap fall short of basic common sense. Lucifer, who had been in the presence of God for many millenniums, would not suddenly fall during a six day creation. The level of depravity that Satan was at when we get to the garden takes much more time than that.

When we get to the garden we find Satan already there and already at the Tree of the Knowledge of good and evil: "*Now the serpent was more subtil than any beast of the field which the LORD God had made"* (Gen. 3:1a). The Bible is clear that this serpent represents Satan:

> *And the great dragon was cast out, **that old serpent, called the Devil, and Satan**, which deceiveth the whole world: he was cast out into the earth, and his angels were cast out with him.* (Rev. 12:9)

> *And he laid hold on the dragon, **that old serpent, which is the Devil, and Satan**, and bound him a thousand years* (Rev. 20:2)

If there was any doubt as to the identity of the serpent, John clears this up for us. When we get to Genesis 3 Satan has already positioned himself as an enemy of God. Here we see that Satan was there performing His work of sin and murder "in the beginning" (John 8:44; 1 John 3:8). He had begun the work of slandering God, telling a bold-faced lie about the consequences of eating the fruit from the tree and manipulating Eve to rebel against the loving command of God.

Some have claimed that God warned Adam against this tree because it was a type of the "tithe" which belonged to God only. It was His desire to teach Adam not to take things that belonged to God only. However, I don't see this as a viable reason for forbidding Adam to take from the tree. Satan was already present at this tree when we come to it. The only obvious reason for this would have to be due to the fact that Satan, just as he did with Job and others, demanded that God allow him to test this new creature. God has to allow such tests for the sake of the one being tested, the watching angels, and for the sake of His own integrity and reputation.

Why the Tree of the Knowledge of Good and Evil?

Why did God place that particular tree in the garden in the first place? In the next chapter we will learn how Satan slandered God and falsely accused Him in order to get the angels to follow him in his rebellion. This slander may have possibly cast doubts in the minds of the other angels concerning God's love, integrity, and justice. Satan was prepared to do this exact same thing with man. Because of His love, God gives men and angels the opportunity to see for themselves whether or not Satan's accusations against Him are true.

When God created man and gave him so much abundance and authority Satan was prepared to accuse Him of bribing these new creatures into loving Him and worshipping Him only for what they can get out of Him. Satan seems to believe that everyone is like him and that all of God's creatures, and even God Himself, are selfish and self-seeking. He was prepared to accuse God of bribery in order to get the worship, love and obedience that He craved. An example of his deceptive tactics is found in the book of Job:

> *And the LORD said to Satan, Have you set your heart against My servant Job, because there is none like him in the earth, a perfect and upright man, one who fears God and turns away from evil? And Satan answered the LORD and said, Does Job fear God for nothing? Have You not made a hedge around him, and around his house, and around all that he has on every side? You have blessed the work of his hands, and his livestock have increased in the land. But put forth Your hand now, and touch all that he has, and he will curse You*

to Your face. (Job 1:8-11; Modern King James Version by JP Greene)

Satan had set his heart against Job and was seeking for a way to destroy him (Eph. 4:27; 1 Pet. 5:8-9). He claimed that Job was worshipping God from a purely selfish motive. He stated that Job only served God because God had *"blessed the work of his hands"*. He was doing the same thing with Adam and Eve since *"....**God blessed them**, and God said unto them, be fruitful, and multiply"*. The tree of the knowledge of good and evil was partly for their protection. As long as they remained loyal to God Satan had nothing upon which he could base an accusation and get an inroad into their lives.

The forbidden tree was also meant to route the attacks of Satan on God's character, thus protecting the faith of His loyal angels. Notice how Satan accuses God of buying Job's worship with all the blessings that God bestowed on him. This is his modus operandi. He was ready to pounce on God before the angelic hosts with this same accusation concerning Adam and Eve. Satan was ready to put doubts in the minds of the angels that had not defected and were still serving God. He was attempting to justify his own rebellion against God and perhaps recruit more angels for his cause.

In order to protect Adam, Eve and the angels from the persuasive lies of Satan, God needed something to shut the accuser's mouth. The tree of the knowledge of good and evil was necessary for this. God has to answer Satan's accusations in order for the universe to understand that Satan is a liar and that God is a fair God. God must allow men and women to freely choose between His government and Satan's government (Joshua 24:15; James 4:7-8; 1 John 3:10).

If men are not able to choose freely then they cannot offer God genuine love and worship. This is what

He desires most. God is not a despot or a dictator. He gives men freedom to make choices for or against Him, but warns of the consequences of making the wrong choice. Satan, on the other hand, desires to enslave and abuse men. However, he knows that he is unable to do so unless men *choose* to submit to his tyrannical reign.

As we have said before, nothing good was withheld from Adam. Even the Tree of Life was accessible to him. He was only forbidden from the *one thing that would hurt him*. In His love, God presents us with wonderful opportunities and nearly begs us to choose against alternatives that bring devastating consequences (Deut. 30:15, 19; John 3:16-18).

Every opportunity to choose obedience to God's Word rather than submission to the enemy is an opportunity to show loving loyalty to God and prove Satan wrong in his false claims against God. Every time we stand on God's promises against Satan's attacks of temptation, sickness, disease, poverty, depression, unforgiveness and other areas in which he attacks these are opportunities to prove how powerful God's Word is in routing satanic destruction.

The Knowledge of Good and Evil

Furthermore, Satan loves to tempt people with "secret" or "forbidden" knowledge. There is a certain amount of pride in having knowledge that is forbidden to others. Why are some of the secret societies such as the Masons and others so successful? Why do some religious orders have people willing to make all necessary sacrifices to reach certain levels that enable them to attain to more and more knowledge?

Satan has planted in the minds of some that forbidden knowledge is to be desired. Yet many who have been a part of such societies and religions but have later found freedom in Christ tell us that these things are demonic. Satan still attempts to persuade people to embrace the knowledge of good and evil in order to be enticed by the evil itself.

Some may not understand what could possibly be wrong with having knowledge of good and evil. Therefore we need to recognize some important truths. First, before Satan ever rebelled, there was no evil in the universe and there was never any need to have knowledge of it. Good (expressed in unselfish love) was the norm. Good and love was taken for granted. Although God is omniscient, even He never seemed to have a need for an intimate knowledge of evil or its possibility (Jer. 7:31; 19:5; 32:35).

Satan introduced the concept of evil into the universe when he first began to introduce to others that there was a way of living, acting, and behaving than the way that God had taught or the knowledge of good that God had placed within His creatures (Ezek. 28:15-18; Gen. 3:1-5).The whole concept of satanic rebellion is to be independent of God. This includes independently knowing the difference between good and evil apart from a knowledge of God. This independence leads people to doing what is right in their own eyes (Judges 17:6; 21:25; Prov. 12:15; 21:2).

The Lie of Independence

Knowledge apart from God leads to the lie of independence. Jesus said, *"I am the vine, ye are the branches: He that abideth in me, and I in him, the same bringeth forth much fruit: **for without me ye can do nothing**"* (John 15:5). Satan's whole temptation to Eve was that she could have the same great wisdom and knowledge that God has without having to depend on God.

> *Now the serpent was more subtil than any beast of the field which the LORD God had made. And he said unto the woman, Yea, hath God said, Ye shall not eat of every tree of the garden? And the woman said unto the serpent, We may eat of the fruit of the trees of the garden: But of the fruit of the tree which is in the midst of the garden, God hath said, Ye shall not eat of it, neither shall ye touch it, lest ye die. And the serpent said unto the woman, Ye shall not surely die: For God doth know that in the day ye eat thereof, then your eyes shall be opened, and **ye shall be as gods, knowing good and evil*** (Gen. 3:1-5)

Satan tempted Eve with the same thing that he wanted: *I will ascend above the heights of the clouds;* ***I will be like the most High*** (Isa. 14:14). Satan's idea was that Eve did not need to learn the truth about good and evil from God. His lie to man was, "Become gods yourself and acquire this knowledge independently." However, this idea of independence is a lie. Knowledge comes from one of two sources:

> *Who is a wise man and endued with knowledge among you? let him shew out of a good conversation his works with meekness of wisdom. But if ye have bitter envying and strife in your hearts, glory not, and lie not against the truth. This wisdom descendeth not from above, but is earthly, sensual, devilish. For where envying and strife is, there is confusion and every evil work. But the wisdom that is from above is first pure, then peaceable,*

> *gentle, and easy to be intreated, full of mercy and good fruits, without partiality, and without hypocrisy.* (James 3:13-17)

Knowledge is power. The one who has the knowledge has the power to direct and control those lacking it. Adam and Eve could choose to get knowledge from Satan which leads to death or from God which knowledge leads to life. Eve saw that it was *"a tree to be desired to make one wise"* (v. 6). What she did not realize was that *"This wisdom ....is earthly, sensual, devilish"*. Sadly she and her husband chose the way of Satan and received his "wisdom".

By yielding to Satan's lie, Adam and Eve certainly got their "independence" but it was much more than they bargained for:

> *Unto Adam also and to his wife did the LORD God make coats of skins, and clothed them. And the LORD God said, Behold, the man is become as one of us,* **to know good and evil***: and now, lest he put forth his hand, and take also of the tree of life, and eat, and live for ever: Therefore the LORD God sent him forth from the garden of Eden, to till the ground from whence he was taken.* (Gen. 3:21-23)

In spite of their rebellion, God lovingly made Adam and Eve clothes. To keep them from a "living death", God removed them from the garden. God said, "Behold, the man is become as one of us, to know good and evil." This meant that man had knowledge of good and evil *apart* from God. Such "independence" separates us from the life-giving knowledge of God (2 Pet. 1:3).

Knowledge from Knowing God

The war between God and Satan is an *information war*. Both God and Satan are fighting for the hearts of men and women through information. It is essential that we know the source of our information. We can choose God as the source of our knowledge or Satan

In Genesis chapter 2 we find God in constant communion with Adam and Eve. No doubt that He took the time to explain to Adam many things. Knowing God's loving nature, there is no beneficial information that He would have withheld from the first couple. God prefers we know *Him* rather than having mere knowledge of good and evil:

> *And this is life eternal, that they might know thee the only true God, and Jesus Christ, whom thou hast sent.* (John 17:3)

> *"Thus saith the Lord, Let not the wise man glory in his wisdom, neither let the mighty man glory in his might, let not the rich man glory in his riches: But let him that glorieth glory in this, that he understandeth and knoweth me, that I am the Lord which exercise lovingkindness, judgment, and righteousness, in the earth: for in these things I delight, saith the Lord."* (Jer. 9:23, 24)

> *"And to know the love of Christ, which passeth knowledge, that ye might be filled with all the fulness of God."* (Eph. 3:19)

When we know God then we will have the knowledge that enables us to reflect His character and nature. God's kingdom is run by agape love. When a person is walking in love, there is need to know the principle of good evil because love automatically does good:

> *For this, Thou shalt not commit adultery, Thou shalt not kill, Thou shalt not steal, Thou shalt not bear false witness, Thou shalt not covet; and if there be any other commandment, it is briefly comprehended in this saying, namely, Thou shalt love thy neighbour as thyself. Love worketh no ill to his neighbour: therefore love is the fulfilling of the law.* (Rom. 13:9-10)

> *But the fruit of the Spirit is love, joy, peace, longsuffering, gentleness, goodness, faith, Meekness, temperance: against such there is no law.* (Gal. 5:22-23)

One can do good without *knowing* evil by simply following the law of love. On the other hand, intimate knowledge of evil often leads to evil acts. For example, many young Children are currently engaging in sexual activity because they have been exposed to this knowledge. The demonic school departments are introducing pornographic material to our youth. Furthermore, the internet and movies are schools of the knowledge of good and evil. Many of our children receive instruction on sex, violence, and other depravity and they often act on this knowledge.

Doing Good without Knowledge of Evil

Mixing the knowledge of good and evil is like mixing toxic poison with delicious healthy food. No one needs to have intimate knowledge of toxic poison in order to know that it will kill you. You simply stay away from it.

One needs no intimate knowledge of evil in order to do good. The angels before Satan's fall knew nothing about evil and served God with bliss and joy for what may have been millions of years without ever knowing the possibility that something called *evil* could ever come into existence. This is a Biblical principle that is true today:

> *Everyone has heard that you do what you were taught, and I am very happy about that. But I want you to be wise about what is good and to* ***know nothing about what is evil*** (Rom. 16:19; Easy to Read Version)

> *People everywhere know that you obey. I am very happy about you. I want you to be wise and know what is right.* ***I want you to know nothing about what is wrong*** (World English New Testament)

This knowledge of Good and evil would not have its source in God but in Satan. Satan gives knowledge of good in a twisted way while enticing a person to evil. Satan would have us attempt to do good without God or His empowerment. Paul's pre-conversion struggle shows us the struggle to do what is right while having knowledge of that which is wrong. The wrong continues to entice us (Rom. 7:7-21).

> *But unto you I say, and unto the rest in Thyatira, as many as have not this doctrine, and which* ***have not known the depths of Satan****, as they speak; I will put upon you none other burden* (Rev. 2:24).

It is not necessary to know the depths of Satan in order to be free of his evil. On the contrary, lack of intimate knowledge of the deep things of the devil probably keeps one from being enticed and falling into his bondage. This is why Jesus commends them for their "ignorance" here.

This is how God wanted Adam, Eve, and the rest of humanity to live. The love and life of God would have been enough. However, Eve, being enticed by Satan, craved something more than was needed, something that lead to her death.

Conclusion

In summary, God restored the earth to a good state after Satan's rebellion. He then created man and gave him authority over His creation. Man was created to work in partnership with God in ruling the world and ridding it of satanic influence. The tree of the knowledge of good and evil was there for man's protection. It was also there to allow him the freedom to choose between God and Satan. Sadly, because man chose "independence" over a loving partnership with God, he abdicated his God-given authority to Satan and became a slave, thus allowing evil to begin its reign anew in our world.

Chapter Four

Why Didn't God Destroy Satan? (Part One)

*Thou hast defiled thy sanctuaries by the multitude of thine iniquities, **by the iniquity of thy traffick**; therefore will I bring forth a fire from the midst of thee, it shall devour thee, and I will bring thee to ashes upon the earth in the sight of all them that behold thee* (Eze. 28:18)

G. H. Pember writes, "For the word translated 'merchandise' [KJV - traffick] may also (as an investigation of the root will show) signify 'detraction' or 'slander'; and we know that the very name 'Devil' means 'the slanderer,' or 'malignant accuser.'"[1] When he rebelled against God, Satan began to engage in slander, thus becoming a *devil*. Lack of love will lead people to slander others.

If there is any "mystery" to evil it is not why God permitted it but how someone could actually have spent centuries in the presence of the kindest, most loving, gracious and patient being in the entire universe and still rebel against Him. How could Satan have rebelled and not realize the devastating consequences of such an act? Even more, why didn't God destroy the devil when he sinned rather than allowing him to continue to pursue his evil activities?

Technically speaking, God has already destroyed the devil through the death, burial and resurrection of Jesus Christ (Heb. 2:14-15; 1 John 3:8). However, "destroy" as used in relation to what Christ did to Satan means that He rendered Satan powerless. In this sense it is referring to the *legal* defeat of Satan and the freedom

Jesus gave us from his tyranny (Acts 26:18; Col. 1:12-14). We will explore this further in chapter eleven.

The question that people are *really* asking when they ask about God destroying the devil is "why did He allow the devil to reign in tyranny in the first place?" Why did He not simply wipe Satan out of existence or at least immediately imprison him in the lake of fire so that He could no longer enforce his evil agenda? Gordon Lindsay summarizes what I believe is the Biblical answer to these sincere questions:

> "The question is: 'Why did God, after the devil rebelled, not punish him at once? Why did He permit him freedom to continue on in his evil course?' Though there is undoubtedly more than one reason why God delayed judgment on Lucifer, the one that surely stands out above others is that Satan in seducing as many as one third of the angels, must have succeeded in bringing into question the goodness and justice of God."[2]

In this chapter we will explore this further as it gives more answers to the reason for evil.

Deceiving the Angels

In order to understand why God did not immediately destroy Satan we need to look at slander and its effects upon the minds of God's creatures. Deception, mixed with slander, has an evil persuasive power. The Bible describes an innumerable amount of angels (Rev. 5:11). Yet, Satan was able to lead a third of them in rebellion against God:

> *And there appeared another wonder in heaven; and behold a great red dragon, having seven heads and ten horns, and seven crowns upon his heads. And **his tail***

> *drew the third part of the stars of heaven, and did cast them to the earth: and the dragon stood before the woman which was ready to be delivered, for to devour her child as soon as it was born.* (Rev. 12:3-4)
>
> *And there was war in heaven: Michael and his angels fought against the dragon; and the **dragon fought and his angels**, And prevailed not; neither was their place found any more in heaven. And the great dragon was cast out, that old serpent, called the Devil, and Satan, **which deceiveth** the whole world: he was cast out into the earth, and his angels were cast out with him.* (Rev. 12:7-9)
>
> *Then shall he say also unto them on the left hand, Depart from me, ye cursed, into everlasting fire, prepared for **the devil and his angels**:* (Matt. 25:41)

How was it that Satan was able to convince so many angels to follow him in rebellion against a great and wonderfully loving God? According to Scripture, Satan, in his fall, became a master of deception. His new found expertise of lying and deceiving was able to persuade others into rebellion.

Satan, who once stood in (held to) the truth, lied in order to win the other angels (and perhaps a preadamite race) to follow him in his rebellion:

> *You belong to your father, the devil, and you want to carry out your father's desire. He was a murderer from the beginning, **not holding to the truth**, for there is no*

> *truth in him. When he lies, he speaks his native language, for he is a liar and the father of lies.* (John 8:44; New International Version)

Satan knew the truth about God and His loving kindness but did not *hold* to it. Gordon Lindsay writes, "Jesus, in His statement concerning the defection of Satan, indicated that the devil deceived the angels".[3] Another author writes:

> "....the father of lies believes his own lies. He had convinced himself that he could defeat the Almighty and usurp Him as God. His plan was to lie his way to the top. If he could create enough problems for God, maybe God would have become discouraged and resign. Maybe if he told enough lies about God, the other angels would doubt Him enough to discontinue worshipping Him."[4]

Satan used deception in an attempt to destroy God's reputation, believing that this would dethrone Him. Sadly, many of the angels bought into it.

Slandering God to the Angels

Strong's dictionary defines the word "devil" as "false accuser, devil, slanderer." Thayer's Greek Definitions expands on this definition: "Prone to slander, slanderous, accusing falsely; a calumniator, false accuser, slanderer; metaphorically applied to a man who, by opposing the cause of God, may be said to act the part of the devil or to side with him."

In his study on this subject, Dr. Robert D. Luginbill translates Ezekiel 28:16 as follows:

> *"In your **extensive conspiring, you were filled with wickedness, and you sinned**. So*

> *I cast you from the mountain of God as one profaned, and I blotted out [your memory] from among the stones of fire, O covering cherub."*

Dr. Luginbill then offers this insight into how Satan was able to persuade numerous angels to follow him into rebellion:

> "Satan's conspiracy is first explicitly mentioned here, that is, his active attempt to carry out his plan of the five 'I wills'. The Hebrew word *rachal* (רכל), translated here as 'conspiring', has the two-fold meaning of repetitive motion ('trading' or 'trafficking') and of slandering. In the context of Satan's activities, it fits our notion of conspiracy quite well. Once arrogance had led to perverted thinking (v.17), these mental attitude sins blossomed into the overt activity of canvassing his fellow angels for support, slandering God in the process, an activity characterized by Ezekiel as 'wickedness'. Satan was attempting to besmirch God's reputation to gain adherents and further his own goals."[5]

Satan was able to deceive the other angels by maligning and slandering God's character. He used lies and deception which has always been a practice with him. This would seem like a good reason for God to be rid of him once and for all. God certainly has the might and power to do it. However, we must keep in mind that God does not operate in mere power alone. He governs the use of His power with His love and wisdom.

Deception and slander lives beyond the deceiver and slanderer. Think of the founders of every major religion, cult, and oppressive system of government. Most, if not all, are dead. Furthermore, these religions and governments have failed to produce the promised results. Yet people continue to believe and adhere to them.

God's primary concern was not to prove that "might makes right." He had to take into consideration the effect of Satan's slanderous lies upon His loyal angels. While two-thirds of the angels may have remained loyal to God, questions may have arisen concerning Satan's accusations against Him.

Absalom: a Picture of Satan's Slander against God

It may help for us to illustrate this truth with another historical incident recorded in Scripture. Some may recall the well-known saying: "History repeats itself". The Bible often records events that parallel other Biblical events. Such is the case of Absalom, King David's son:

> *But in all Israel there was none to be so much praised as Absalom for his beauty: from the sole of his foot even to the crown of his head there was no blemish in him.* (2 Sam. 14:25)

Now compare the description of Absalom to the description of Satan (Lucifer) in Eze. 28:12-13. We are told that Lucifer was *"perfect in beauty."* We also read, *"....there was none to be so much praised as Absalom for his beauty."* Two creatures who were made beautiful forgot the One who created them this way and began to take pride in their gifts.

The comparisons between Lucifer and Absalom are even stronger, as if Absalom's story was written to describe exactly how Lucifer went about his deception of the angels in the beginning of his fall. Absalom, like Lucifer did with the angels, began to sway those coming to the king by insinuating that he was a better governor:

> *And Absalom said unto him, See, thy matters are good and right; but there is no man deputed of the king to hear thee. Absalom said moreover,* ***Oh that I were made judge in the land, that every man which hath any suit or cause might come unto me, and I would do him justice!*** *And it was so, that when any man came nigh to him to do him obeisance, he put forth his hand, and took him, and kissed him. And on this manner did Absalom to all Israel that came to the king for judgment: so Absalom stole the hearts of the men of Israel.* (2 Sam. 15:3-6)

Absalom, who was certainly under Satan's influence to begin with, demonstrates how Satan deceived other angels to side with him. Like Satan, Absalom offered something that he claimed his father was *not* giving. Absalom used "conspiracy" (Treason):

> *And Absalom sent for Ahithophel the Gilonite, David's counsellor, from his city, even from Giloh, while he offered sacrifices.* ***And the conspiracy was strong;*** *for the people increased continually with Absalom.* (2 Sam. 15:12)

Now compare the above with Rev. 12:3-4 in which Satan was able to use deception to draw a vast amount of angels to side with him against God. Two thirds of an innumerous host of angels is a large amount to deceive.

Absalom was able to use *slander* against his father's government in order to win over a portion of the people. To make matters worse, Absalom started a war with his father that he quickly lost (Compare 2 Sam. 17:1-4 with Rev. 12:7-9). Absalom was, like Satan, able to accomplish all of this because he was able to place doubt in the minds of the angels about God.

Satan Slanders God Concerning Job
The book of Job also provides us with a picture of Satan's slandering tactics and how he still attempts to prove his case. Satan's tactic is seen in that he still attempts to place doubt about God's loving character in the minds of the remaining loyal angels.

> *And a day came when the **sons of God** came to present themselves before the LORD. **And Satan also came among them**.* (Job 1:6; Green's Modern KJV)

The "sons of God" mentioned in the above passage are God's remaining loyal angels: *"When the morning stars sang together, and all the **sons of God** shouted for joy?"* (Job 38:7). Daniel also writes:

> *He answered and said, Lo, I see four men loose, walking in the midst of the fire, and they have no hurt; and the form of the fourth is like the **Son of God**.... Then Nebuchadnezzar spake, and said, Blessed be the God of Shadrach, Meshach, and Abednego, **who hath sent his angel**, and delivered his servants that trusted in him....* (Dan. 3:25, 28a)

Notice how Satan knew when the rest of the angels were reporting to God and came among them. We also see that that Satan came with an agenda:

And the LORD said to Satan, From where do you come? Then Satan answered the LORD and said, From going to and fro in the earth, and from walking up and down in it. And the LORD said to Satan, Have you set your heart against My servant Job, because there is none like him in the earth, a perfect and upright man, one who fears God and turns away from evil? **And Satan answered the LORD and said, Does Job fear God for nothing?** *Have You not made a hedge around him, and around his house, and around all that he has on every side? You have blessed the work of his hands, and his livestock have increased in the land. But put forth Your hand now, and touch all that he has, and he will curse You to Your face. And the LORD said to Satan, Behold, all that he has is in your power. Only do not lay your hand upon him. And Satan went forth from the presence of the LORD.* (Job 1:7-12; Green's Modern KJV)

For years theologians have told us that Job was all about God's agenda (that he was using Satan to test Job). However, when this book is read carefully we can see that it is really about Satan's agenda to malign God's character.

Satan is still attempting to persuade as many more angels as he can to rebel against God. He attempts to raise doubts in their minds about God's character. Notice how Satan accuses God of *buying* Job's worship. He claims that no one will love God sincerely. They only serve Him for what they can get from Him.

Satan tries to convince the council that God is not governing the universe properly and that he could do a better job. He attempts to prove it at Job's expense. Satan knows that he cannot physically do any harm to God so he instead does to God's image (Gen. 1:26-28) what he would like to do to God Himself.

From Job we get a glimpse of how Satan made his first attempt to slander God and was successful with one third of the angels. We also get an understanding of how God Himself chooses to vindicate His reputation. In their excellent book, *"God's Strategy in Human History,"* Marston and Forster relate this incident to the reason why God could not just merely remove Satan from existence:

> Why God didn't immediately destroy Satan when challenged concerning Job: "We must be clear exactly what we mean if we say that God 'could have stopped' Job's suffering. We may indeed accept that he had the sheer power to stop or even destroy Satan. The problem is that in this case, even as Satan sank under God's wrath and destruction, he would have gone down with a sneer on his lips as though to say, 'I told you so.' Such a 'solution' would have left forever unanswered Satan's accusation that God's kingdom was based (like his own) on force and expediency. It was not lack of power that prevented God from crushing Satan – it was a matter of principle…. Satan's accusations must be answered, and they cannot be truly answered by a force that simply crushes the accuser."[6]

I believe that Marston and Forster's assessment is accurate. Slander lives beyond the slanderer. Short of God simply destroying every creature who begins to doubt His love (which would prove Satan's point that God is an overbearing egotistical dictator who demands His own way—*or else!*) God's only response to Satan's allegations is to allow him the opportunity to prove to the watching universe if his accusations against God have merit. God cares more about His creatures worshipping Him from love, free of doubts, than from fear of retribution.

Slandering God to Eve

Satan's tactics are also seen in how he slandered God to Eve. After God created man, Satan successfully won them to his side by using slander:

> *Now the serpent was more subtil than any beast of the field which the LORD God had made. And he said unto the woman, Yea, hath God said, Ye shall not eat of every tree of the garden? And the woman said unto the serpent, We may eat of the fruit of the trees of the garden: But of the fruit of the tree which is in the midst of the garden, God hath said, Ye shall not eat of it, neither shall ye touch it, lest ye die. And the serpent said unto the woman, Ye shall not surely die: For God doth know that in the day ye eat thereof, then your eyes shall be opened, and ye shall be as gods, knowing good and evil.* (Gen. 3:1-5)

Gordon Lindsay writes, "But now to consider the means that Lucifer used to deceive the angels. We can certainly learn something about this from a study of how he deceived Eve."[7] Take note of Satan's attacks on God. First, Satan attacked God's **character of love** by accusing Him of selfishness. Satan insinuated that God is arbitrary and unkind in forbidding the fruit of this one tree.

Secondly, Satan attacked God's **character of goodness** by accusing Him of selfishly withholding from Eve (in spite of the generosity of allowing the couple to eat from every tree of the garden except *one*). Finally,

Satan attacked God's **character of honesty** by accusing Him of lying when He told Adam that eating from the tree would *certainly* result in death. However, God does not forbids sin in order to hold us down but because *it destroys* (Rom. 5:12; 6:23; James 1:15). The Bible describes Satan's actions towards Adam and Eve as "deception:"

> *And Adam was not deceived, but the woman **being deceived** was in the transgression.* (2 Tim. 2:14)

> *But I fear, lest by any means, **as the serpent beguiled Eve through his subtilty**, so your minds should be corrupted from the simplicity that is in Christ.* (2 Cor. 11:3)

Sadly, Adam committed his sin in light of true knowledge. He knew better and still gave in to Satanic temptation. Satan is still tempting and deceiving today. His primary means of temptation is to slander God before men and angels in the hopes of them joining his rebellion. As E. M. Bounds aptly stated:

> "Satan is blasphemous, arrogant, and presumptuous. He slanders God to men and infuses into their minds distorted thoughts about God. He intensifies their hatred and inflames their prejudice against Him. He leads them to deny God's existence and to misrepresent His character, thereby destroying the foundations of faith and all true worship."[8]

Along with the elect angels, mankind also needs to see that God is nothing like the way Satan has made Him out to be. This is why God cannot immediately destroy Satan.

Chapter Five

Why Didn't God Destroy Satan? (Part Two)

*Thou hast defiled thy sanctuaries by the multitude of thine iniquities, **by the iniquity of thy traffick**; therefore will I bring forth a fire from the midst of thee, it shall devour thee, and I will bring thee to ashes upon the earth in the sight of all them that behold thee* (Eze. 28:18)

In the last chapter we saw from Scripture how Satan was able to use deception and slander in order to persuade at least a third of the angels to follow him in his unsuccessful rebellion against God. We learned from several Biblical incidents his method of slander and its power to cast doubt upon the minds of those who hear it.

From this truth we begin to see why a loving God cannot merely do away with Satan. Slander lives beyond the slanderer. If God immediately destroyed Satan upon his rebellion this would not have resolved the issue of His reputation. On the contrary it would have exacerbated the problem. Once Satan is gone then there is no way for God to prove that he was wrong, thus leaving doubt in the minds of His loyal angels.

God Needs Time to Vindicate Himself

Seeing that God has been slandered by Satan and Satan's destruction would only leave doubt lingering against God for the rest of eternity, God needs time to vindicate Himself. In His Word God assures us that Satan's tyranny will soon end. God has a set time in which He will deal with him. In Revelation we read:

> *Therefore rejoice, ye heavens, and ye that dwell in them. Woe to the inhabiters of the earth and of the sea! for the devil is come down unto you, having great wrath, **because he knoweth that he hath but a short time.*** (Rev. 12:12)

Although there are a number of interpretations of the book of Revelation, I believe that most of the events recorded in them are futuristic. Understanding these events as *futuristic* helps us to see that evil will not reign in God's universe forever. The agent and engineer behind evil has only a short time left. An incident in which Jesus confronted some demons while He was on earth tells us that there is an appointed time for Satan's demise:

> *And when he was come to the other side into the country of the Gergesenes, there met him two possessed with devils, coming out of the tombs, exceeding fierce, so that no man might pass by that way. And, behold, they cried out, saying, What have we to do with thee, Jesus, thou Son of God? **art thou come hither to torment us before the time?*** (Matt. 8:28-29)

Rest assured that Satan and demons will reap heavily the misery that they have sown among God's creation. They recognize that this time is coming. When they saw God approach them in human flesh they thought that they were about to get an early start. When their final end comes, it will not be an enjoyable situation. Instead it will be eternal endless torment:

> *And the devil that deceived them was cast into the lake of fire and brimstone, where*

> *the beast and the false prophet are, and* **shall be tormented day and night for ever** *and ever.* (Rev. 20:10)

Satan's torment will be for an eternity. He will suffer far more than the suffering he has dispensed (and that is saying a lot). However, in order for God to allow him to suffer so immensely for an endless period of time, God must prove that He is fully justified in bringing this about. Otherwise He will be accused of meanness and cruelty for the rest of eternity.

God is just and fair even to someone as evil as Satan. By the time Satan is finally punished, the universe will have seen that God has been more than fair to Satan, having given him plenty of time to either repent or prove his case against God.

What is God Waiting For?

Why didn't God destroy the devil and his followers immediately? Why wait? Why does God still allow Satan and his evil forces to roam the earth torturing and tormenting? Why not get this "lake of fire" deal done and over with?

Destroying Satan would only make his slanders against God seem plausible to the faithful angels and to His other creatures. He would appear to be a tyrant who destroys those who oppose Him. God does not rule through intimidation and fear, but through love:

> *Herein is our love made perfect, that we may have boldness in the day of judgment: because as he is, so are we in this world. There is no fear in love; but perfect love casteth out fear: because fear hath torment.* **He that feareth is not made**

> ***perfect in love.*** *We love him, because he first loved us.* (1 John 4:17-19)

> *That he would grant unto us, that we being delivered out of the hand of our enemies might **serve him without fear**, In holiness and righteousness before him, all the days of our life.* (Luke 1:74-75)

God is not a tyrannical ruler who demands service for fear of punishment. God wants *children*. He wants *love relationships*. If God had destroyed Satan then the angels would have served Him from *fear* rather than *reverential love*.

> *So you should not be like cowering, fearful slaves. You should behave instead like God's very own children, adopted into his family – calling him "Father, dear Father."* (Rom. 8:15; New Living Translation)

Serving someone from fear is a life of torment. There is no pleasure in it. Many of us have either lived through oppressive governments, spousal abuse, schools, parents, or even work environments where fear was the norm. Our only thought was how to escape from it. Others merely lived with the hopelessness of such a situation. God does not desire this for His own. He wants eternity to be filled with joy and happiness, free from fear. This could not happen if doubts remain about His own character.

Furthermore, the universe needs to see that ruling through evil simply does not work. Once the universe has seen the results of evil and its final outcome, rebellions will cease. If God had immediately destroyed Satan and the angels who rebelled, it would have left questions in the minds of the loyal angels regarding Satan's accusations. Now all of God's creatures have a first-hand view of how "evil" evil is. Once it is gone no one will ever want it back because they will have seen its fruit.

Did Satan Think he Could Succeed?

Satan's rebellion against an omnipotent God brings up other questions that are worth examining. For example, why did Satan think that his rebellion would succeed against an omnipotent God? The answer goes right back to *the love of God*. Although Satan knew that God is all-powerful, he counted on the fact that God is not a tyrant who stops rebellions through destruction. Dr. Luginbill writes:

> "How ironic it is that Satan, who knew much better than we the awesome power of God, has been relying all along **on the character of God** to protect him from the wrath of God! No doubt he thought to put God in an insoluble dilemma: either tolerate the breach in universal order and harmony or rend unity and peace forever by crushing Satan. Satan counted on God's tolerating evil rather than taking an irrevocable step that would permanently mar His creation."[1]

I agree with Dr. Luginbill. Look again at Job 1:6: *"And a day came when the **sons of God** came to present themselves before the LORD. **And Satan also came among them**"* (Green's Modern KJV). If God were a tyrant like Satan, and like the picture that Satan often paints of God to angels and to men, then he would not dare approach Him. However, Satan failed to understand that within the laws of the moral universe that there is an inherent consequence to sin (Matt. 25:41; Rev. 20:10).

Can Satan Repent?

Another question often asked by many (and one that I also asked at one time) is, "If Satan were to repent, would God forgive him?" Some who hold to doctrines of "universalism" and "ultimate reconciliation" have unbiblical fantasies about God reconciling everyone back to Himself, to include Lucifer. However, if this were true then God has shown Himself to be more cruel than one can imagine as He allows all of this meaningless suffering to go on when the agents who bring the suffering really have no will of their own. After all, He would have to override the freedom of will of these heinous rebels in order to force their reconciliation.

Beloved, unless repentance is an act of one's will, it is not true repentance. Therefore, universalism and ultimate reconciliation are not sensible solutions, nor are they consistent with the plain teaching of Scripture. Calvinism and predestination theology teaches the false idea that God ordained Satan's rebellion and evil from eternity past. It was in His predestined plan for Satan to fall and cause all of this misery and Satan's final demise has also always been a part of God's predestined plan. Hence Satan will not repent because God did not include that in His plan. This idea is even more wicked than universalism.

The Biblical answer is that Satan's desire to repent (or lack thereof) has nothing to do with God. Men and angels who persist in sin sooner or later, of their own doing, get beyond the ability to repent. They become so hardened in their sin that God cannot do anything apart from violating their will (Psalm 81:12; Hosea 4:17; Rom 1:28-32; 1 Tim. 4:2; 2 Tim. 3:13; 1 John 5:16; Rev, 22:11). The problem is not with God. Forgiveness and mercy is His nature and character (Psalm 86:5; 145:8-9; Dan. 9:9; Micah 7:18). He gives plenty of time to repent:

> *The Lord is not slack concerning his promise, as some men count slackness; but is longsuffering to us-ward, not willing*

> *that any should perish, but that all should come to repentance.* (2 Pet. 3:9)

Concerning "Jezebel" (a false prophetess in the early church) Jesus said:

> **'I gave her time to repent, and she does not want to repent of her immorality.** *'Behold, I will throw her on a bed of sickness, and those who commit adultery with her into great tribulation, unless they repent of her deeds.* (Rev. 2:20-22; New American Standard)

Due to His nature, God would have given Satan much time to repent. However, Satan became hardened as men do today, and was beyond the ability to repent.

> *Now the Spirit speaketh expressly, that in the latter times some shall depart from the faith, giving heed to seducing spirits, and doctrines of devils; Speaking lies in hypocrisy;* **having their conscience seared with a hot iron** (1 Tim. 4:1-2)

> *Ephraim is joined to idols: let him alone. Their drink is sour: they have committed whoredom continually: her rulers with shame do love, Give ye. The wind hath bound her up in her wings, and they shall be ashamed because of their sacrifices.* (Hosea 4:17-19)

God attempts to reach out and reason with sinners (Prov. 1:24-30; Isa. 1:18-20; 65:2, 12; 66:3-4; Zech. 7:11-12). However, sinners reject His love so God eventually has to "give them over" to a reprobate mind (Rom. 1:28-32; Psalm 81:11-12). When someone is bound in sin then there is no desire to repent and there is nothing that God can do for them. To prove this point further so that there is never a doubt in anyone's mind concerning God's justice, Jesus will have Satan bound for 1000 years and then released again. This will prove that Satan's character is so malignant that he could never repent:

> *And he laid hold on the dragon, that old serpent, which is the Devil, and Satan, and bound him a thousand years, And cast him into the bottomless pit, and shut him up, and set a seal upon him, that he should deceive the nations no more, till the thousand years should be fulfilled: and after that he must be loosed a little season... And when the thousand years are expired, Satan shall be loosed out of his prison, And shall go out to deceive the nations which are in the four quarters of the earth, Gog and Magog, to gather them together to battle: the number of whom is as the sand of the sea.* (Rev. 20:2, 3, 7, 8)

Some have wondered why God is going to only lock Satan up for a millennium and then release him again before final punishment. It is a valid question. Theodore Epp Explains:

> "Why is it necessary to loose Satan after the 1000 year rule of Christ? ....it will prove he is still the same after the 1000 years of imprisonment. His evil nature will not change simply because he is confined for 1000 years. This demonstrates the justice of God in His final, eternal judgment of Satan."[2]

A. B. Simpson also gives some great insight:

> For 6,000 years he has been permitted to rule, and the result is desolation, sorrow, death and desperate ruin. Now for 1,000 years Christ has reigned and he beholds a prospect of beauty, blessedness and peace. How can he fail to recognize the difference between the evil and the good, and, if there can be one spark of desire in his fallen spirit, to turn toward the light? This is the final opportunity. Who can tell whether, if even he had learned the lesson of his long and dreadful imprisonment, had appreciated the meaning of this blessed object lesson of righteousness, and had turned to Jehovah with repentance and sincerity, even he might have found some place of mercy.[3]

This is the answer to the often asked question about Satan's ability to repent and whether or not God would forgive him. Satan is a "hardened criminal." He is the persona of evil. He has become so hardened in his hatred against God that no repentance or reconciliation is remotely possible at this point. But for the sake of the creatures He loves, God will go out of His way to prove this point. It will be seen that the problem with Satan's repentance does not rest with God but with Satan.

On a practical note, we must all be careful about indulging and remaining in sin. Continued rebellion hardens a person to the place where they will not come to God to receive mercy even though God is always willing to dispense it. Therefore, *"To day if ye will hear his voice, harden not your hearts"* (Heb. 3:15).

Understanding God's Character

The angels, especially through the redemptive work of Christ, have come to understand the truth about God and the clear evidence that Satan is a liar:

> *Unto whom it was revealed, that not unto themselves, but unto us they did minister the things, which are now reported unto you by them that have preached the gospel unto you with the Holy Ghost sent down from heaven;* **which things the angels desire to look into.** (1 Pet. 1:12)

It seems that the redemptive work of Christ has such an effect on the angels of God that they worship Him concerning this:

> *And I beheld, and* **I heard the voice of many angels** *round about the throne and the beasts and the elders: and the number of them was ten thousand times ten thousand, and thousands of thousands; Saying with a loud voice,* **Worthy is the Lamb that was slain** *to receive power, and riches, and wisdom, and strength, and honour, and glory, and blessing.* (Rev. 5:11-12)

Satan accused God of selfishness. However, God the Son made an unselfish sacrifice on mankind's behalf and helped the angels see that He is *worthy* of worship.

Satan often attributes to God his own selfish characteristics. Often, a husband who cheats on his wife will accuse his wife and others of cheating. Many people inflect their own faults upon others. Satan was the first to do this and became the master of it. Part of the war between God and Satan is for God to show the world that He is not the way that Satan has described Him. What Satan accuses God of being and doing is actually Satan doing it.

Chapter Six

Why Does the Bible Attribute Evil to God?

> *Let no man say when he is tempted, I am tempted of God: for* **God cannot be tempted with evil, neither tempteth he any man***.... Every good gift and every perfect gift is from above, and cometh down from the Father of lights, with whom is no variableness, neither shadow of turning* (James 1:13, 17)

> *So listen to me, you who can understand. God can never do wrong!* ***It is impossible for the Almighty to do evil*** (Job 34:10; New Century Version)

> *This then is the message which we have heard of him, and declare unto you, that* ***God is light, and in him is no darkness at all*** (James 1:5)

The Bible uses "light" and "good" as well as "darkness" and "evil" synonymously (Job 30:26; Isa. 5:20; John 3:19-20). The description of God as being light with no darkness at all means that there is not even an iota of evil within Him. Furthermore, darkness is always attributed to the kingdom of Satan (Acts 26:18; 2 Cor. 4:3-4; Eph. 6:10-12; Col. 1:12-14).

Nonetheless, other areas of our English Bibles seem to place a lot of blame on God for many of the evil incidents that take place in the historical accounts of His people. This is especially true of the Old Testament though this is not completely absent from the New.

We cannot accept some portions of the Bible as the divinely inspired Word of God but reject other portions. It is either all the Word of God or none of it is. I believe without question that the entire Bible is God's inspired Word. Yet how do we reconcile passages attributing evil to God with those that reveal His character as one without any evil? In this chapter we offer you the Biblical solution.

God is not the Author of Evil

Before exploring the reasons why the Bible appears to attribute so much evil to the hand of God we need to ground ourselves in some foundational Biblical truths concerning God's character. We must grasp the fact that God is not the source of any type of evil—physical or moral.

James says that God is the "Father of lights." A "father" is one that produces from the seed that is already in him. Since God is good then He is unable to do anything that constitutes as evil:

> ***Even so every good tree bringeth forth good fruit***; *but a corrupt tree bringeth forth evil fruit.* ***A good tree cannot bring forth evil fruit****, neither can a corrupt tree bring forth good fruit* (Matt. 7:17-18)

God is exceedingly good (Psalm 25:8; 34:8; 86:5; 106:1; 107:1; 118:1, 29; 119:68; 135:3; 136:1; Mat. 19:17). Therefore He can only produce that which is good. All that is wrong and hurtful does not come from His hand. That's why James says that, *"Every* **good gift** *and every* **perfect gift is from above***, and cometh down from the Father of lights."* God is good and therefore is unable to give that which is evil:

> *Or what man is there of you, whom if his son ask bread, will he give him a stone?* ***Or if he ask a fish, will he give him a serpent?*** *If ye then, being evil, know how to give good gifts unto your children, how much more shall* ***your Father which is in heaven give good things to them that ask him?*** (Matt. 7:9-11)

Notice that Father-God can only dispense good gifts. He does not give or tempt people with evil. Evil is not in Him, therefore He cannot give it or create it. When God created (or restored) the earth, everything was good (Gen. 1:3-31). Now contrast this with the fatherhood of Satan:

> *Ye are of your father the devil, and the lusts of your father ye will do. He was a murderer from the beginning, and abode not in the truth, because there is no truth in him. When he speaketh a lie, he speaketh of his own:* ***for he is a liar, and the father of it*** (John 8:44)

Satan is the "father" of murdering and lying. As a "father" Satan can only bring forth evil fruit. Jesus said in Matt. 15:19, *"For out of the heart proceed evil thoughts, murders, adulteries, fornications, thefts, false witness, blasphemies."* This is all that is in Satan's heart and this is all that he is able to produce.

The Bible refers to Satan as the prince (ruler) and god of this world (Luke 4:5-6; John 12:31; 14:30; 16:11; Eph. 2:1-2; 6:10-12; 2 Cor. 4:4). He is the one who holds sway and control over it (1 John 5:18-19). There is no wonder that Scripture refers to this world and its works as evil (Isa. 13:11; John 3:19; 7:7; Gal. 1:4). Therefore Father-God vindicates Himself when we are told,

> *For all that is in the world, the lust of the flesh, and the lust of the eyes, and the pride of life,* **is not of the Father,** *but is of the world* (1 John 2:16)

God is not the source of any of the evil that we find in our world. All evil has its source in Satan. The picture of God that is sometimes given to us by many theologians is one of a very dark being. It is this being that is opposed by atheists and drives them away from God. A true understanding of God will demonstrate that there is nothing that the average person understands as being "darkness" is found in God.

Eastern Idiom of Permission

But again, we find many Old Testament (and some New Testament) passages attributing evil to God. Why is this so? With very little attention given to Satan in the Old Testament (see next chapter for more details), there is a scarce information as to the cause of evil. Apart from a well understood teaching about the existence of the forces of darkness the Hebrews were forced to adopt the Ancient Near Eastern idioms to which everything that happens is attributed to the ruling deity, even if that deity was not the cause of the incident. These are what we call "permissive idioms".

The problem with the majority of English translators has been the failure to translate these cultural idioms. As John Hale Murray notes:

> One peculiarity of the Hebrew tongue is that it abounds in figures of speech that must necessarily be understood, to gain its intended meaning. The simple mode of life in which the earliest Israelites lived, doubtless made them great observers of nature; any reference to which, from their

> familiarity with it, made them require no explanations. Our difficulty here is to reconcile this with our ideas and language; and the neglect of these idioms with our translators, where they have given a literal verbal translation, without the customary sense of the original, has led them into many errors.[1]

Murray provides an excellent example of how the neglect of this idiom this idiom has made God appear to be the author of horrendous evil to include incest and rape. After David's adultery and subsequent murderous act God says through the prophet Nathan:

> *Thus saith the LORD, Behold,* ***I will raise up evil against thee*** *out of thine own house, and I will take thy wives before thine eyes, and give them unto thy neighbour, and he shall lie with thy wives in the sight of this sun* (2 Sam. 12:11)

God says that *He will raise up evil*. Yet, we have just learned from other passages of Scripture that God is not the source or author of evil. If God does not tempt with evil and He is not the source of evil then how is He able to raise up evil? Furthermore, Bible readers know that Nathan's prophecy saw its fulfilment when David's son, Absalom, rebelled against his father and raped his wives publicly (2 Samuel 16:21-22).

Sadly, many atheists have used these passages to prove that the God of the Bible is immoral. Many of our theologians have been no help to God's cause since they have promoted a version of "sovereignty" that actually makes God the first cause of all that happens. John Hale Murray noted how some of the church's most well-known and revered theologians have unwittingly charged God with egregious evil because they neglected to consider this Eastern idiom of permission when interpreting passages such as 2 Sam. 12:11:

> Our translation here represents God as the author of evil, which made Calvin say that "the incest of Absalom was the work of God." "Thus saith the Lord, behold I will raise up evil against thee—I will take thy wives, and give them .... and he shall lie with them." In the original these expressions do not denote any positive actions on the part of God, as if he prompted wicked men to do the things with which he threatened David. This would indeed be to make God the author of evil. He meant that, as a punishment to David, God would withhold his restraint from David's enemies, because David had grossly violated God's laws. God permits the evils to be done which his omnipotence could prevent; and does not, in certain cases, restrain the wickedness of men, in their being the means of chastising the sins of his own people.[2]

Here we see that God is not the source of any of the evil that came upon David and his household. David opened the door for these evils to come upon his home when he committed some terrible sins. God allowed David to "reap what he had sown" by not preventing the sowing and reaping process from taking its course. Yet, apart from understanding the permissive idiom within the Hebrew language and culture, the literal translation will confuse many Bible readers and God is charged with being the source of evil when He says in other places that He has nothing to do with it.

God is not the Source of Physical Evil

Some of our scholars understand that much of what David suffered in his family were moral failures and would wholeheartedly agree that God has nothing to do with it. However, many of them do not share that perspective as it relates to *physical* evil. Some theologians like to make distinctions between *moral* and *physical* evil and then claim that, though God is not the source of *moral* evil, He does bring sickness, disease, death and natural catastrophe.

However, the same permission idioms relate to both *moral* and *physical* evil. The best example of this is in the book of Job. Job, as far as we know, had no moral failures. Yet he suffered a number of physical evils to include the tragic loss of his children and property, natural disasters, and even sickness. Job attributes all of this to the hand of God:

> *Then said his wife unto him, Dost thou still retain thine integrity? curse God, and die. But he said unto her, Thou speakest as one of the foolish women speaketh. What?* **shall we receive good at the hand of God, and shall we not receive evil?** *In all this did not Job sin with his lips* (Job 2:9-10)

So many people have read Job's statement and have misused it to bring "comfort" to others who have suffered loss and tragedy. Job is not at fault for his statement because he had no knowledge of what was actually occurring in the spirit realm. Furthermore, it was the nature of his culture to attribute every event to God if God did not prevent the event from taking place. However, readers of the book of Job should be more careful than to attribute this evil to "the hand of God" since we are clearly told in Job 1 that this all came from the hand of Satan:

> *Hast not thou made an hedge about him, and about his house, and about all that he hath on every side? thou hast blessed the work of his hands, and his substance is*

> *increased in the land. But put forth thine hand now, and touch all that he hath, and he will curse thee to thy face. And the LORD said unto Satan,* **Behold, all that he hath is in thy power**; *only upon himself put not forth thine hand. So Satan went forth from the presence of the LORD.* (Job 1:10-12)

In Job 2:6 we read, *"And the Lord said unto Satan,* **Behold, he is in thine hand***; but save his life."* While Job ascribes these evils to God's hand God Himself clearly reveals that they came from the hand of Satan. Basically, when Job attributes the evil he suffered as being "the hand of God" Job is merely ascribing to God as *doing the thing which He only permitted.*

God is only said to have brought evil to Job because He removed His hand of protection, something that He did reluctantly. Satan had just accused God of buying Job's worship and accused Job of only worshipping God for what he could get from God. Satan denies that anyone has unselfish motives.

The most perplexing thing about Job 2:9-10 is how so many people quote it in an effort to comfort those who are sick, who lost a child, or experienced some other tragic event. It is almost as if they forgot to read the chapter and verses before Job's statement. God is not the source of any of the physical evils that Job suffered. He merely permitted them though He later overturned them (Job 42:10-11; James 5:11).

God did not Create Evil

Another passage that has stumped some and have led others into erroneous assumptions about God is a well-known passage in Isaiah:

> *I form the light, and create darkness:* ***I make peace, and create evil****: I the LORD do all these things.* (Isa. 45:7)

Based on this passage some have declared that God is the creator of all darkness and evil. Did God actually create evil as He did the earth, the heavens, angels, animals, and humans? Can evil even be considered a created thing? Such an idea contradicts other Scriptures concerning the nature and character of God.

The Bible also makes it implicitly clear that God hates evil and that He has absolutely nothing to do with it (Psalm 5:4; Prov. 8:13; Jer. 44:4-5; Prov. 6:16-19; Zech. 8:17; Deut. 28:31; Hab. 1:13; Job 34:10-12). So why does God say that He is the creator of darkness and evil in Isa. 45:7? This is resolved as we continue to learn the *language of the Bible.* To understand the problem of evil we must again understand the Hebrew language and its "permissive idioms". Just as we saw in 2 Sam. 12:11 and Job 2:9-10 the language in Isa. 45:7 must be viewed as "permissive" rather than "causative". Victor Alexander, a native Aramaic speaker, offers this this translation of Isaiah 45:7 from the Aramaic Scriptures:

> "He [God] who forms light and creates the dark, Who makes peace and lets evil happen; I am the Maryah who did all these things."[3]

In a footnote Alexander expounds further: "Makes peace and creates [or allows] evil." NB! "To create or allow evil is not the same as 'doing evil.'"[4] An Old Testament scholar, Dr. Walter C. Kaiser, is also helpful:

> Even though much of the physical evil often comes through the hands of wicked men and women, ultimately God permits it. Thus, the Hebrew way of

speaking, which ignores secondary causation in a way Western thought would never do, whatever God permits may be directly attributed to him, often without noting that secondary and sinful parties were the immediate causes of the disaster....
It is God who must allow (and that is the proper term) these calamities to come.[5]

Hence Isaiah 45:7 should be understood as permissive on God's part rather than causative. Evil is the result of people removing themselves from God's protection, thus receiving the consequences of their choices in a morally ordered universe. God's responsibility as far as evil is concerned is only to the extent that He created laws of sowing and reaping.

Just like the other passages above that ascribe evil to God, Isa. 45:7 must be understood from a "permissive" rather than a "creative" sense. In Deuteronomy 28:15-28 a lot of "punitive" language is ascribed to God. God is said in this passage to bring about the results of disobedience. God, speaking through Moses personally ascribes to Himself the tragedies that would fall upon Israel such as *"I will destroy thee.... I will smite thee....I will send enemies.... I will send pestilence... etc."*

However, these are simply Hebrew idioms which ascribe to God as doing the thing which He only permitted. Interpreting Scripture with Scripture, we see that God is not the author of the disasters (evils) that came upon Israel. He *permits* these disasters due to their sin:

> *And the Lord said unto Moses, Behold, thou shalt sleep with thy fathers; and this people will rise up, and go a whoring after the gods of the strangers of the land, whither they go to be among them,* **and will forsake me, and break my covenant** *which I have made with them. Then my*

anger shall be kindled against them in that day, **and I will forsake them, and I will hide my face from them**, *and they shall be devoured,* **and many evils and troubles shall befall them**; *so that they will say in that day,* **Are not these evils come upon us, because our God is not among us?** *And* **I will surely hide my face** *in that day for all the evils which they shall have wrought, in that they are turned unto other gods.* (Deut. 31:16-18).

The word "evils" in the passage above is the Hebrew word "ra"; the same word used in Isa. 45:7. Interpreting Scripture with Scripture we see that evil comes when the Lord is *absent*. The removal of God's protection (when He forsakes His people) allows those things His presence previously protected the people from to take place. However, when God removes His protection He takes responsibility for what happens afterwards as if He personally caused it. This is the proper understanding of the phrase "I create evil".

Translating Permissive Verbs as Causative

One more truth we should briefly note is the fact that some of the permissive verbs in the Hebrew were incorrectly translated in a causative sense into the English language. For example when King Ahab chose to listen to false prophets rather than a true prophet of God we are told:

Now therefore, behold, the Lord hath **put a lying spirit** *in the mouth of all these thy prophets, and* **the Lord hath spoken evil concerning thee** (1 Kings 22:23)

We learned earlier that Satan, not God, is the "father of lies" (John 8:44). Yet, here we are told that God *put* a lying spirit in the mouths of Ahab's false prophets. The word "put" in verse 23 is the Hebrew word *"nathan"* which is actually translated in most passages of Scripture in a "permissive" sense. One theologian writes:

> *"The Lord hath put a lying spirit in the mouth of all these thy prophets."* This is the common translation, "But the original Hebrew does not sanction such a rendering. For it makes Jehovah the author of this sin, by exerting an influence over the minds of the idolatrous priests to persuade Ahab to ascend to Ramoth-gilead, that he might destroy him." "The word *naathan,* is rendered *hath put* i.e. *the Lord."* But it is perfectly proper that the passage should receive the same rendering, as in other places.[6]

If we persist in rebellion and we persist in believing lies, then God is obligated to permit us to have the very thing we have chosen (2 The. 2:10, 11; Rom. 1:24-28). But God is not the One who sends these deceivers (Jer. 14:15; 23:32; 29:31). Therefore when the Hebrew word *"nathan"* that has been translated "put" in 1 Kings 22:23 is properly translated as "allow" or "permit" then the passage should read, *"....the LORD hath **permitted** a lying spirit in the mouth of all these thy prophets."* God simply permitted what Ahab already wanted.

Understanding this and the other truths above helps us understand how to read the Bible in a way that is free from making God the cause of evil. The Bible only attributes evil to God in the *permissive* sense—when He does not use His power and authority to prevent the evil. In this sense God is said to do that which He merely allowed or permitted.

Chapter Seven

Why is Satan Absent in the Old Testament?

> …. throughout the Old Testament there is a development of doctrines in the line of clearer expression and additional instruction as the book advances. This is true of the doctrine of Satan as well as of others which became more fully unfolded as the worship of Jehovah was more firmly established.[1] – William Matson

For verily I say unto you, That many prophets and righteous men have desired to see those things which ye see, and have not seen them; and to hear those things which ye hear, and have not heard them. (Matt. 13:17)

Satan is not entirely absent from the Old Testament but admittedly his name does not pop up as frequently as it does in the New. Not all of the truth concerning God's character, angels, Satan, demons, and the universe was given to the Israelites in the beginning. God revealed truth to His people only when there was a purpose for it and if He knew that they could handle it.

As we read through the Bible starting with Genesis on to the New Testament, we notice a development of understanding about many things. This is what a number of Bible scholars have referred to as "progressive revelation." Due to revelation progressing through the centuries, idioms were employed by the Hebrews to explain things that God had not yet fully revealed.

The Necessity of Progressive Revelation
God did not give His revelation progressively out of a desire to hide truth from people or to be mysterious and secretive. God attempted to reveal enough truth about Himself and the nature of evil using the idiomatic language available. He left enough information in the Scriptures to help the diligent seeker. Scripture tells us, *"It is the glory of God to conceal a thing: but the honour of kings is to search out a matter"* (Prov. 25:2).

Those who really wanted to know the truth could have searched it out and discovered it. However, God concealed things because He knew people would not be able to handle certain truths due to sin having dulled their minds (Matt. 13:10-15). The same is true of the idiomatic language used in much of the Bible, especially the Old Testament. Since many of the people of those times were not ready for a full understanding of God's truths, He spoke to them using language that they would be able to comprehend.

Progressive Scientific Understanding
Some examples of this are found in the knowledge of science and the workings of the universe among the Hebrews. The Jewish people used idiomatic language concerning the sun:

> *For from the rising of the sun even unto the going down of the same my name shall be great among the Gentiles; and in every place incense shall be offered unto my name, and a pure offering: for my name shall be great among the heathen, saith the Lord of hosts* (Mal. 1:11)

God, using the idiomatic expression of His people, spoke about the sun "rising" and "going down". Today we know that the sun does not "rise" or "go down". God has allowed scientists to discover that He created the earth to orbit around the sun. The earth spins (or rotates) on its axis towards the east, giving the effect of a sun rising and falling from our perspective.

It is not that scientists today are smarter than the ancients. The Old Testament people were not so "primitive". They simply did not possess the means to understand all of these things at the time and God had no special need to explain all the workings of the universe in its full detail. Furthermore, despite our current knowledge of science, we still use these same idioms in which we make reference to a "sunrise" and a "sunset".

This lack of detailed knowledge did not prevent God from acting on Israel's behalf nor did it prevent Israel from accomplishing its mission as in Joshua's case (see Joshua 10:12-14).

Furthermore, the Bible appears to some to teach a flat earth since, in some places, it is described as having "four corners" (Isa. 11:12; Rev. 7:1). Many of the ancient people believed that the earth was flat. Yet, the Bible always explains its own language in other places. For example, in Isaiah, the same book that speaks about the earth having four corners also says, *"It is he that sitteth upon the circle of the earth"* (Isa. 40:22a). The Jamieson-Fausset-Brown Bible Commentary says that this circle is, "applicable to the **globular form** of the earth"[2] (emphasis mine)

Progressive Knowledge of Satan

Some may find it silly that anyone would interpret idiomatic language literally to insist on a flat earth, a rising and setting sun, and live in fear of falling off into space. Yet many of these same people do just that with other portions of the Bible, particularly where God is said to have performed some horrible act such as sending evil spirits, deception, sickness, disaster, suicide, and other evil events.

Apart from understanding progressive revelation and why all truth about God's character was not crystal clear in earlier books of the Bible, we paint a picture of a God who scares us rather than One we want to embrace in love. God often took responsibility for many Old Testament incidents due to His need to reveal Satan's kingdom progressively. Just as with scientific information that we take for granted today, the Israelites were not ready for a full disclosure of these truths concerning Satan's kingdom. As some scholars have stated:

> "Since there is no developed picture of a devil or satan in most of the Old Testament, God takes responsibility for everything, even for evil he might have prevented. God stands above opposing deities; his power is unsurpassable, according to the Hebrew Bible. And in that world of competing deities and rival religions, absolute control was essential. In other words, in order to meet ancient Israelites in terms they could understand in their world, God takes ultimate responsibility."[3]

Though Satan is not absent from the Old Testament, there was not a full understanding of his role in relation to evil and its consequences during the earliest period of Old Testament times. This knowledge was given progressively. Therefore, there is some truth to the fact that God often took credit or responsibility for some of Satan's acts as well as His other creatures. However, just as He did with the "flat earth" idioms, He always explains the language used immediately in the context of the passage (Compare 1 Chron. 10:13 with verses 3-6) or elsewhere in Scripture (Compare 2 Sam. 24:1 with 1 Chron. 21:1).

As to the agency of evil and Satan's part in it, we can see that he was not fully revealed from the beginning.

In Genesis 3 we are told that it was the serpent that deceived and tempted Eve:

> *Now the serpent was more subtil than any beast of the field which the Lord God had made. And he said unto the woman, Yea, hath God said....* (Gen. 3:1-2)

There is no mention of Satan here. Yet it is not difficult to see the antagonism towards God in the serpent's words. The serpent maligns God's character by painting Him as an egotistical liar bent on His own self-preservation. He claims that God is holding back from Adam and Eve to avoid competition. From the very beginning of things we learn that God has an enemy.

However, through progressive revelation we can easily identify who the serpent is. Paul tells the Corinthians that he is concerned about their giving themselves over to satanic deception: *"But I fear, lest by any means, as the serpent beguiled Eve through his subtilty, so your minds should be corrupted from the simplicity that is in Christ"* (2 Cor. 11:3). Paul then explains who the deceiving serpent is:

> *For such are false apostles,* ***deceitful workers****, transforming themselves into the apostles of Christ. And no marvel;* ***for Satan himself is transformed into an angel of light****. Therefore it is no great thing if his ministers also be transformed as the ministers of righteousness; whose end shall be according to their works* (2 Cor. 11:13-15)

In Paul's epistle we learn how the serpent is connected to the ultimate deceiver which is Satan. Paul was concerned that Satan would use the false apostles influenced by Satan to corrupt the minds of the Corinthians just as he did with the serpent in Eden.

Apostle John also makes a clear connection to the serpent in Genesis being the representation of Satan. In his vision of Jesus ushering in His millennial reign John tells us that he saw an angel who *".... laid hold on the dragon, **that old serpent, which is the Devil, and Satan**, and bound him a thousand years"* (Rev. 20:2). John said that it is this serpent that is at war with God, men, and God's loyal angels:

> *And there was war in heaven: Michael and his angels fought against the dragon; and the dragon fought and his angels, and prevailed not; neither was their place found any more in heaven. And the great dragon was cast out, **that old serpent, called the Devil, and Satan**, which deceiveth the whole world: he was cast out into the earth, and his angels were cast out with him.* (Rev. 12:7-9)

In the New Testament we have a clear revelation of Satan as the serpent. Satan through a murderous intent, was promoting his lies against God in order to destroy man "in the beginning" (John 8:44; 1 John 3:8. Compare to Matt. 19:4, 8; Mark 10:6; 2 Pet. 3:4).

In the beginning God had given man authority over the earth and all of the works of His hands (Gen. 1:26-28; Psalm 8:5). The serpent succeeded in bringing about the fall of man which allowed Satan to legally usurp the man's authority (Luke 4:4-5; Rom. 5:12-14; Heb. 2:14-15). Part of the redemptive work of Jesus was to recover from Satan the authority that man had lost (Matt. 28:18-20; Rev. 1:18).

In Gen. 3:14-15 we read where God warns the serpent about someone who would come to crush his head (the place of power). Later centuries would reveal that this was a warning to Satan that the second member of the triune Godhead would destroy him through His sacrificial redemptive work on behalf of man (Luke 10:17-19; Rom. 16:20; 1 Cor. 15:25-28).

One other thing worthy of mentioning is the fact that Satan is revealed as "the great dragon" in the Revelation passages cited above. In scattered parts of the Old Testament we find God defeating dragons such as Leviathan and Rahab (Job 41:1; Psalm 74:13-14; 89:10; 91:13; 104:26; Isa. 27:1; 51:9). It is only in the New Testament that the dragon is completely identified as Satan.

Progressive Revelation Concerning Cain

The progressive nature of revelation concerning Satan is also seen in the historical account of Cain killing Abel. In Genesis 4 both Cain and Abel offered sacrifices to God. Abel's sacrifice was offered in faith and was better than Cain's (Heb. 11:4). Cain, on the other hand, offered God fruit that came from a ground that had been cursed (Gen. 3:17-18). This made Cain angry. God warned Cain that there is a *personality* out waiting to destroy him:

> *And the LORD said unto Cain, Why art thou wroth? and why is thy countenance fallen? If thou doest well, shalt thou not be accepted? and if thou doest not well,* **sin lieth at the door***. And unto thee shall be his desire, and thou shalt rule over* **him** (Gen. 4:6-7)

God uses personal pronouns such as "his" and "him" when describing sin to Cain. He speaks of sin as a *personality*. Cain ignored God's loving admonition. He allowed sin to rule over him and murdered Abel. Early readers of this book may not have necessarily identified the personality of *sin* that moved Cain to murder his brother as Satan. John later identifies that the devil was the personality that God was referring to in Genesis:

> **Not as Cain, who was of that wicked one**, *and slew his brother. And wherefore slew he him? Because his own works were evil, and his brother's righteous.... Whosoever hateth his brother is a murderer: and ye know that no murderer hath eternal life abiding in him* (1 John 3:12, 15)

John makes it clear that Cain opened the door to the "wicked one," which is another title for Satan and the devil (Compare Matt. 13:19 to Luke 8:12 and Mark 4:15).

We have this knowledge due to the progress of revelation throughout the Scriptures. The first readers of Genesis probably did not understand that Satan was the personality behind Cain's murderous nature. However, the New Testament reader has a clear knowledge of this truth.

Progressive Revelation Concerning Demonology

Another area in which revelation was progressive is the source and influence behind evil spirits. The Old Testament saints were fully aware of evil spirits (demons) (Lev. 17:7; Deut. 32:17; 2 Chron. 11:15; Psalm 106:37). However, in several cases in Scripture these demonic entities are said to have come from God to punish wayward individuals. One example is found in the case of

Saul in which we are told that he received an evil spirit *from the Lord*:

> *But the **Spirit of the Lord <u>departed</u> from Saul, and an evil spirit <u>from the Lord</u> troubled him.** And Saul's servants said unto him, Behold now, an evil spirit from God troubleth thee. Let our lord now command thy servants, which are before thee, to seek out a man, who is a cunning player on an harp: and it shall come to pass, when the evil spirit from God is upon thee, that he shall play with his hand, and thou shalt be well* (1 Sam. 16:14-16; see also v.23; 18:10-12; 19:9; 28:15-18).

Apart from understanding the progressive nature of revelation, there have been not a few people who have accused God of being personally involved in someone's demon possession.

Adolphus Frederick Schauffler writes, "It only remains to say that there is need of no other agency from God than the permissive. Satan never needs to be sent on such a mission; it is only requisite that the Lord suffer him to go."[4] Walter Scott states that Saul's experience should be read in light of the Ancient Near Eastern Hebrew idiom of permission:

> "We are told, in the same verse, that the Spirit of God departed from Saul. This must mean that the Holy Spirit withdrew his influence, and, consequently, Saul lost the gifts, the ability for government, and managing the affairs of his kingdom, which had been imparted to him, when 'the Spirit of God came upon him, and he became another man,' 1 Sam. x. 6. Does it not follow from this, that the tempers which he afterwards manifested, were the effects of the influence of an

evil spirit, opposite to the Spirit of God? And, as it came upon him in consequence of the withdrawment of the Divine Spirit, and by the permission of the Divine Being, and also as a judgment, it may, with the greatest propriety, and especially in the Hebrew idiom, **according to which God is often said to do that which he permits to be done, and renders subservient to his purposes, be represented as from God.** This is the natural interpretation of the passage, and that which best agrees with the general doctrine of the Bible respecting evil spirits."[5] (Emphasis are mine)

God said to Hosea, *"....woe also to them when I depart from them!"* (Hosea 9:12b). When God departs it means that He has withdrawn His protection over the person and Satan is given full access (Matt. 18:34; 1 Cor. 5:1-5; Eph. 4:26-27; 1 Tim. 1:20). When the Spirit of the Lord departed from Saul he was left without divine protection from Satanic onslaughts (Luke 11:24-26).

We are warned not to give any place to the devil through our sin (Eph. 4:24-27; 2 Cor. 2:10, 11; 2 Tim. 2:24-26; 1 Pet. 5:8). When we persist in sin God will turn us over to Satan (Matt. 18:32-35; 1 Cor. 5:1-5; 1 Tim. 1:20). This implies removing His protection from over us and allowing Satan to have his way (Job 1:9-12). Jesus later reveals that these demons were under Satan's authority and were part of a kingdom that is at war with God's kingdom (Matt. 12:22-26).

Is God a Tempter?

Due to the fact that God had to allow revelation to progress, He spoke using the idioms of the people by which He took credit for the things that He merely permitted. A clear example is found in 1 Samuel 24:1:

> *And again the anger of the LORD was kindled against Israel, and he moved*

> *David against them to say, Go, number Israel and Judah* (2 Sam. 24:1)

The word "moved" in this passage in the Hebrew is "by implication to seduce" (Strong's Concordance). The New Testament is clear that God does not seduce men to sin:

> *Let no man say when he is tempted, I am tempted of God: for God cannot be tempted with evil, neither tempteth he any man"* (James 1:13)

So how do we explain what appears to be an apparent contradiction between the Old Testament understanding of God's dealings and the New? *The first thing is to remember that there is no contradiction.* Second, go completely with the picture of God as revealed in the New Testament.

Once you accept the New Testament's testimony concerning God's character then you can go back to other passages in the Old Testament that sheds more light on the problematic passage. In the case of God seducing David to sin, 1 Chron. 21:1 gives us the interpretation we need: *"And Satan stood up against Israel, and provoked David to number Israel"* While God took responsibility for David's enticement to sin, the New Testament reveals that God does not *personally* tempt any man. Thankfully 1 Chron. 21:1 explains the idiomatic language used in 2 Sam. 24:1.

Scholars say that 2 Samuel was written in 1120 BC and 1 Chronicles was written several centuries later between 450BC to 400 BC. Ezra the Scribe is credited with having written 1 Chronicles and we believe He wrote it by the inspiration of God (2 Tim. 3:16). Henry Cowles writes, "It may, perhaps, be put to the account of 'progress of doctrine' that in the later book (Chronicles) this agency is ascribed to Satan, while in the book of Samuel, neither his name nor his agency appears."[6]

Cowles refers to "progress of doctrine" as the reason that we do not discover until centuries later that Satan was behind the temptation that David suffered. The progress in revelation helps us to understand why Satan appears to be absent from most of the Old Testament (though he is not) and why God took responsibility for numerous things described as "evil."

The Bible describes Satan as the tempter (Matt. 4:1-3; 1 Thess. 3:5). God is not the seducer but the One who helps to escape trials tests, and temptations (Luke 11:4; 1 Cor. 10:13). He took credit for many of these things in the Old Testament until He could give further light. It is now our obligation as New Testament believers to study from this light now given.

Chapter Eight

Why Did God Create if He Knew?

> If God did not purpose man should sin (and Calvinists now, in words deny He did) then He was frustrated when Adam fell. There is surely no mystery about the fall this far.[1] – Robert Plues

Why did God create this world if He knew that things would turn out this way? Did God want any of this to happen? Did He know that it would happen? There are some who believe that God wanted the world to fall into sin and desired the spread of evil. They believe that He had a secret plan.

God's Plan or He Just Knew?
Many who follow the teachings of the 16th century reformer, John Calvin, believe that God wanted all of this to happen. John Calvin wrote, "For the first man fell because the Lord had judged it to be expedient; why he so judged is hidden from us."[2] Calvin believed that God wanted man to fall and for "mysterious" purposes. Calvinist Edwin Palmer makes it even plainer:

> All things that happen in all the world at any time and in all history—whether inorganic matter, vegetation, animal, man or angels (both good and evil ones—come to pass because God ordained them, Even sin- the fall of the devil from heaven, the fall of Adam, and every evil thought, word, and deed in all of history.[3]

Many have rightly opposed these teachings. However, those opposed to Calvinism repudiate it with the idea that "God foreknew that angels and men would fall because

He is outside of time and can see the past, present, and future all at once. However this was the best world out of all of the possible worlds He could have created so He chose to create this one." For the most part, it is claimed by these theologians to be a "mystery" as to why He created the world knowing that billions, perhaps, trillions, would suffer eternal damnation due to the evil that took place when angels and men fell.

Man is Culpable for what he Knows

Both views described above have in common the idea of "mystery" concerning God's relationship to evil and both are espoused in pulpits, books, commentaries, Sunday school (or "Sabbath school" if you are part of some of the seventh day denominations) literature and other periodicals.

While many Christians have accepted one or the other of these views and are unconcerned about resolving the "mysteries" inherent in them, others are a little stumped by this. How can God not be at fault for bringing about a world with so much evil and suffering if He ordained that it would take place or if He knew, based on His exhaustive foreknowledge, that the creation would become evil? How could He not be at fault for the multitude of people who are suffering in hell today? Doesn't God Himself hold men responsible for committing an act that they knew would lead to harm? Note these parables of Jesus:

> *And that servant,* **which knew his lord's will, and prepared not himself***, neither did according to his will, shall be beaten with many stripes.* (Luke 12:47)

> *His lord answered and said unto him,* **Thou wicked and slothful servant, thou**

> *knewest that I reap where I sowed not, and gather where I have not strawed: Thou oughtest therefore to have put my money to the exchangers, and then at my coming I should have received mine own with usury* ....*cast ye the unprofitable servant into outer darkness: there shall be weeping and gnashing of teeth.* (Matt. 25:25-27, 30)

In these parables we see that God holds people accountable for doing something or failing to do something based on the knowledge that they had. Is God right for holding men responsible for this? In the account in which King Saul has turned against David, Jonathan assures David that he would have acted appropriately if he had known what was to take place in David's life:

> *Therefore thou shalt deal kindly with thy servant; for thou hast brought thy servant into a covenant of the LORD with thee: notwithstanding, if there be in me iniquity, slay me thyself; for why shouldest thou bring me to thy father? And Jonathan said, Far be it from thee:* ***for if I knew certainly that evil were determined by my father to come upon thee, then would not I tell it thee?*** (1 Sam. 20:8-9)

Jonathan assured David that he would take action if he had knowledge of evil that would come upon David. Furthermore, God tells people that they should have taken a different direction than they did to avoid certain problems and/or accrue certain blessings (2 Sam. 12:8; Isa. 48:18; Jer. 23:22; Matt. 11:21-23; 12:7; John 4:10). If God advises people in this manner, would He have gone against His own wisdom in creating creatures He knew beyond a shadow of a doubt would bring devastating evil, suffering and damnation into the universe?

Even the "world rulers" (Satan and his fallen angels – Eph. 1:1-5; 6:10-12) would not have killed Jesus if they had known that it would bring about their defeat:

> *But we speak the wisdom of God in a mystery, even the hidden wisdom, which God ordained before the world unto our glory: Which none of the princes of this world knew:* **for had they known it, they would not have crucified the Lord of glory.** (1 Cor. 2:7-8)

Are wicked creatures wiser than God in taking a different course of action in light of more sufficient knowledge?

Is God Negligent?

If God created with full foreknowledge of the evil that would infiltrate man and eternally damn the majority of them then this makes Him reckless, negligent, and fully culpable for the evil. To have perfect knowledge that an action taken, regardless of how noble it may be, would lead to the death and eternal damnation of millions, perhaps even billions, of people, as well as provide the opportunity for horrendous evil to take place, makes the actor just as responsible for the evil as if he or she is the one that committed the actual evil.

For example, a scientist creates a virus because he believes that a certain strain of it can cure some diseases, but if released upon society as a whole, he has full knowledge that it will kill billions. But for the good of a few who can get cured from other diseases, he releases this virus into public. Is he not reckless and culpable?

Not too long ago I watched a documentary where a married woman and her pastor (who was also married) were having an affair. The pastor wanted to marry the woman but knew that divorce would hurt his reputation and he could not continue to pastor. The married woman gave him the combination to the safe where her husband kept his gun. The pastor went into the safe, got the gun and killed her husband. She was given 8 years jail time because she knew that her act would lead to the death of another even though she did not personally shoot him.

To say that God had a right to create with full knowledge of the fact that His creatures would release horrendous evil into the universe is no different than this woman's actions. Furthermore, it is similar to saying that David's actions against Uriah were justified or that Ahab's actions against Naboth the Jezreelite were justified. Concerning David we read:

> *Wherefore hast thou despised the commandment of the LORD, to do evil in his sight? thou hast killed Uriah the Hittite with the sword, and hast taken his wife to be thy wife, and hast slain him with the sword of the children of Ammon.* (2 Sam. 12:9)

In the example above, David did not lay a hand on Uriah, but he created the circumstances with full knowledge of what was going to happen. God says that it is the same as having murdered Uriah himself. This same truth is applied to Ahab's sin against Naboth (1 Kings 18:17-19). Ahab did not lay a hand on Naboth. His wife manipulated circumstances that caused Naboth to be stoned. But God held Ahab responsible because he knew about it and could have prevented it.

Neither King David nor King Ahab had a personal hand in these murders but they created the situations by which these men would be murdered knowing full well what would take place, and God held them accountable for their actions.

Some argue that foreknowledge of events does not make God anymore responsible for them than our after-knowledge of them. However, this is a fallacious argument. If I have full knowledge of a coming disastrous event and I have the power to stop it but fail to do so then I am criminally negligent and responsible for those destroyed in the disaster. After-knowledge, on the other hand is done and over with. Contrary to time travel fiction, there is no undoing the past, not even for God.

However, the future can be changed if one possesses omnipotent power and has exhaustive foreknowledge of it. As we will see, God denies possessing exhaustive foreknowledge of future events. Therefore He cannot be blamed for the evil that came about in His good creation. Those who assign Him exhaustive foreknowledge denigrate His character and make Him the author of evil.

God is not to Blame

One cannot be blamed for what they did not know. The Lord judged Eli because he *knew* what his sons were doing and made no attempt to stop them:

> *Then the LORD said to Samuel, "I am going to do something in Israel that will make the ears of everyone who hears it ring. On that day I am going to do to Eli and his family everything I said from beginning to end. I told him that I would hand down a permanent judgment against his household* **because he knew about his**

sons' sin—that they were cursing God — but he didn't try to stop them. (1 Sam. 3:11-13; God's Word Translation)

Does God have double-standards? If God knew from all eternity past that Eli's sons would act this way, but punish Eli for his knowledge, then this makes God one of the worse hypocrites. Yet, Scripture shows us differently:

Therefore, the LORD God of Israel declares: **I certainly thought that your family and your father's family would always live in my presence.** *But now the LORD declares: I promise that I will honor those who honor me, and those who despise me will be considered insignificant.* (1 Sam. 2:30; God's Word Translation)

You cannot prevent what you did not know. That is why God forbade punishing parents for the sins of their children (Deut. 24:16; 2 Kings 14:6; Eze. 18:1-4). No parents should be responsible for their child later becoming a criminal nor should God be blamed for creating those who later, of their own choice, became evil.

An Open View of the Future

If God preplanned everything, including evil, then that makes Him the author of evil. Most might reject the idea that God preplanned evil but many still believe that He created the universe knowing that evil and devastation would occur. But what if God actually did *not* know?

From 1 Sam. 2:30 above God tells Eli *"I thought your family ....would always be in my presence."* This means that God never knew the sinful outcome of Eli and his sons until they continued in unrepentant sin.

There is no denying that God is ominiscient (e.g., I Chr. 28:9; Job 24:23; 31:4; 34:21; Psl. 119:168; 139:23-24; Jere. 16:17; 17:9-10; Lk. 16:15; Acts 1:24; Rom. 8:27; 1 Cor. 4:5; 1 Jn. 3:19-20). However, the knowledge described in the passages above does not necessitate that God has detailed knowledge of every single decision that every person will ever make in life. Finis Dake in his excellent book, *God's Plan for Man*, explains:

> God knows His plan from the beginning to the end, and certain passages used to teach foreknowledge from all eternity in connection with detailed events in the lives of free wills really refer to His general plan only, not to free moral acts of those particular men.... (Isa. 42:9; 45:11; 46:9; 48:6; Dan. 2:28, 29; Acts 15:18; Matt. 13:35; 24:36; Rev. 21-22; etc.)[4]

We believe that when this Biblical truth is understood, it will vindicate God from all charges of having brought evil into the universe and place the blame squarely on the responsible parties – the devil and mankind. Scripture reveals that God did not know that Satan would become so monstrous when He created him. God actually *discovered* iniquity in him:

> *Thou art the anointed cherub that covereth; and I have set thee so: thou wast upon the holy mountain of God; thou hast walked up and down in the midst of the stones of fire. Thou wast perfect in thy ways from the day that thou wast created,* **till iniquity was found in thee**. (Eze. 28:14-15)

The word "found" is the Hebrew word *"matsa'"*. According to **Vine's Complete Expository Dictionary** it means "to discover".[5] If God knew before Lucifer was created that he would become evil then why use language implying that He later *discovered* evil in him? It is obvious that if God *discovered* iniquity in Lucifer then it was not something that was foreknown. It was something that became known at the time that it was discovered.

Furthermore, God did not know that man would rebel and bring devastation and ruin into the world. God gave a clear command to Adam and expected him to obey it. There is no good or legitimate reason for Adam to have done other than what he was commanded. Yet he did exactly the opposite. Contrast what God said about the creation (or restoration) of the world in Genesis 1 with what He discovers some generations later:

> *Then God said, "**Let us make humans in our image, in our likeness**. Let them rule the fish in the sea, the birds in the sky, the domestic animals all over the earth, and all the animals that crawl on the earth."*
> *....**And God saw everything that he had made and that it was very good**. There was evening, then morning—the sixth day.* (Gen. 1:26, 31; God's Word Translation)

> ***The LORD saw how evil humans had become on the earth***. *All day long their deepest thoughts were nothing but evil.* ***The LORD was sorry that he had made humans on the earth, and he was heartbroken***. *So he said, "I will wipe off the face of the earth these humans that I created. I will wipe out not only humans, but also domestic animals, crawling animals, and birds.* ***I'm sorry that I made them***.*"* (Gen. 6:5-7; God's Word Translation)

God is not at all responsible for the condition of the world that we find in Genesis 6. John wrote, *"For all that is in the world, the lust of the flesh, and the lust of the eyes, and the pride of life, **is not of the Father**, but is of the world"* (1 John 2:15-16). John's Spirit inspired statement could not be true if God either ordained this evil or He foreknew it would all happen. The Biblical truth is that man is fully culpable for these conditions: *"For as by one man's disobedience many were made sinners"* (Rom. 5:19; see also 1 Sam. 15:22-26; Eph. 5:1-6; Col. 3:1-12; 1 Tim. 1:8-10).

If God knew that man would disobey Him and become evil then why did He pronounce them "good" in the beginning? Why does He become sorry and heartbroken later when they become so evil? None of this makes any sense if God foreknew that men would be evil when He created them. As Gordon C. Olson wrote, "While therefore, there was the possibility of Adam's fall, there were thousand s of probabilities to one that he would be obedient."[6]

It Never Entered God's Mind

Genesis 6 is not the only time in recorded Biblical history that God has expressed regret for a decision He has made (see 1 Sam. 13:13-14; 15:10-11). This is because God's free-will creatures can actually do things that He never thought that they would do. Does God know every act and decision beforehand? God says that certain evil things that people did never entered His mind:

> *They have built worship sites at Topheth in the valley of Ben Hinnom in order to burn their sons and daughters as sacrifices. I did not ask for this. **It never entered my mind.*** (Jer. 7:31; GWT)

> *They have built worship sites to burn their children as sacrifices to Baal. I didn't ask them or command them to do this.* ***It never entered my mind.*** (Jer. 19:5; GWT)
>
> *In the valley of Ben Hinnom they built worship sites for Baal to sacrifice their sons and daughters to Molech. I didn't ask them to do this.* ***It never entered my mind. I didn't make Judah sin.*** (Jer. 32:35; GWT)

God says that He never commanded Israel to sin (KJV), asked them to do it, or made them do it. What they did never entered into His mind nor did He know it. While this goes against commonly held notions about God, it is a Biblical truth that is emphasized repeatedly in Scripture.

God's Disappointment with His Creation

Denial of exhaustive foreknowledge is not a common teaching within the church. Therefore, bear with me as I give you just a few more Scriptures out of the many we could cite here. In these passages you will find that God was often disappointed since He expected His people to do what was right. But they did evil instead:

> *And now, O inhabitants of Jerusalem, and men of Judah, judge, I pray you, betwixt me and my vineyard. What could have been done more to my vineyard, that I have not done in it? wherefore, when I looked that it should bring forth grapes, brought it forth wild grapes?* (Isa. 5:3-4)

> When Josiah was king, the LORD asked me, "Did you see what unfaithful Israel did? She went up every high mountain and under every large tree, and she acted like a prostitute there. **I thought that after she had done all this that she would come back to me. But she didn't come back**, and her treacherous sister Judah saw her. (Jer. 3:6-7; GWT)

> "I wanted to treat you like children and give you a pleasant land, the most beautiful property among the nations. **I thought that you would call me Father and wouldn't turn away from me. But like a wife who betrays her husband, so you, nation of Israel, betrayed me**," declares the LORD. (Jer. 3:19-20; GWT)

> As a belt clings to a person's waist, so I have made the entire nation of Israel and the entire nation of Judah cling to me," declares the LORD. "I did this so that they would be my people and bring fame, praise, and honor to me. However, they wouldn't listen. (Jer. 13:11; GWT)

God is disappointed because He wanted a certain outcome but received something different. God neither causes evil nor does He create with a full foreknowledge that it will take place. *Biblically*, God did not foresee the fall of Lucifer or man. Hence God is not culpable for the evil that has taken place in the universe. Men and devils are fully responsible for it. Thankfully, God has a plan to someday bring it to a complete end.

Chapter Nine

Why Doesn't God Intervene and Stop Evil?

And he said unto them, When ye pray, say, Our Father which art in heaven, Hallowed be thy name. Thy kingdom come. Thy will be done, as in heaven, so in earth (Luke 11:2)

You have seen the picture of the starving children and the drought-filled lands where people and cattle are dying. You have watched the news where nations are destroying each other through war. You have heard about the Christians being tortured and killed in Communist and Islamic countries.

Perhaps you did not need to hear about any of these since you were and still may be a victim of horrendous evil yourself. Perhaps you have a sickness, you are near death, or you have a loved one who is painfully suffering and dying. Perhaps you are just suffering a heavy overwhelming trial right now.

The questions we ask in the face of numerous types of evil can be, "Where is God in all of this? Why doesn't He do something about it? Why is He allowing so much suffering?" These are not questions so much about God's character but inquiries as to why God, who is good, all powerful and full of love for His creation, does not intervene to help in the midst of so much horrible suffering.

Two Kingdoms in Opposition

One recurring theme you may notice in this book is the fact that God gave man dominion over the earth (Gen. 1:26-28; Psalm 8:5-6). Man, in turn, sold out his dominion to Satan through sin (Luke 4:5-6; Rom. 5:12; 1

John 3:8; 5:18-19). Though Satan's time is short, God must honor the covenant He made with man (Rev. 12:9-11). Therefore, God desperately needs man's cooperation if He is to intervene on the earth.

This is why Jesus tells us to pray, *"Thy kingdom come. Thy will be done, as in heaven, so in earth."* Contrary to the belief of some, this is not a prayer of submission to whatever happens on the earth. The picture that some have of a dark and cruel God who forces sickness, poverty, and tragedy upon people and then make them pray such a prayer is worse than any known dictator recorded in history. This is *not* the God of our Lord Jesus Christ.

We are praying *"Thy kingdom come. Thy will be done, as in heaven, so in earth"* because there are two kingdoms operating in this world that are opposed to each other and are at war with each other. Paul writes, *"Who hath delivered us from the power of darkness, and hath translated us into the kingdom of his dear Son"* (Col. 1:13). Paul tells us that it is this dark kingdom that we are at war with:

> *Put on the whole armour of God, that ye may be able to stand against the wiles of the devil. For we wrestle not against flesh and blood, but against principalities, against powers, against the* **rulers of the darkness of this world**, *against spiritual wickedness in high places* (Eph. 6:11-12)

Note that God is not controlling the events in this world. Through His servant Paul God reveals that Satan and his angels are the ones ruling the darkness of this world. Jesus explains the vast difference between the nature of Satan's kingdom and that of His own:

And Jesus knew their thoughts, and said unto them, Every kingdom divided against itself is brought to desolation; and every city or house divided against itself shall not stand: And if Satan cast out Satan, he is divided against himself; **how shall then his kingdom stand?** *And if I by Beelzebub cast out devils, by whom do your children cast them out? therefore they shall be your judges.* **But if I cast out devils by the Spirit of God, then the kingdom of God is come unto you** (Matt. 12:25-28)

Satan has a kingdom and it is one of demonic oppression and darkness. All of the poverty, sickness, famine, drought, slavery, persecution, murder, and anything else that hurts and destroys is his doing. Jesus says that you will know that His kingdom has come upon us when we experience deliverance from the tyranny of Satan.

Therefore to pray, *"Thy kingdom come. Thy will be done, as in heaven, so in earth"* is to ask, as Jesus stated here in Matthew 12 to know *"....then the kingdom of God is come unto you"* as we experience deliverance from satanic oppression. Paul told us that part of our warfare with the rulers of darkness is, *"Praying always with all prayer and supplication in the Spirit"* (Eph. 6:18).

God Needs us to Intervene

One of my favorite authors, S. D. Gordon wrote, "The earth is in a state of war. It is being besieged and so one must use war talk to grasp the facts with which prayer is concerned. Prayer from God's side is communication between Himself and His allies in the enemy's country."[1] Gordon further writes:

> Now prayer is this: A man, one of the original trustee class, who received the earth in trust from God, and who gave control over to satan; a man on the earth, the poor old satan-stolen, sin-slimed, sin-cursed, contested earth; a man, on the earth, with his life in full touch with the Victor, and sheer out of touch with the pretender-prince, insistently claiming that Satan shall yield before Jesus' victory, step by step, life after life. Jesus is the victor and Satan knows it, and fears Him. He must yield before His advance, and he must yield before this man who stands for Jesus down on the earth.[2]

In other words, God needs one of His blood-bought children on the earth to invite His kingdom reign in order to route the works of darkness in the lives of men. Far from submitting to the evil prevalent in this world, we are to stand against it through the Word of God and prayer. When we pray, *"Thy kingdom come. Thy will be done, as in heaven, so in earth"* we are acknowledging that God's will is not always done on the earth. His will depends upon the prayers of His committed blood-washed saints in order for it to be accomplished. It is *asking with authority* that the will of God in Heaven be accomplished on the earth. Jesus said:

> *Verily I say unto you, Whatsoever ye shall bind on earth shall be bound in heaven: and whatsoever ye shall loose on earth shall be loosed in heaven. Again I say unto you, That if two of you shall agree on earth as touching any thing that they shall ask, it shall be done for them of my Father which is in heaven* (Matt. 18:18-19)

Notice the parallels in "The Lord's Prayer" and His prayer instructions above. In "the Lord's Prayer" we are to address *"Our Father which art in Heaven."* In Matthew 18 we are told, *"....any thing that they shall ask, it shall be done for them of my Father which is in heaven."* We are addressing the Father in Heaven who will do what is needed on earth. His will is done in Heaven and He will act to make His will happen on the earth when we ask.

Furthermore, we see the parallel between *"Thy will be done in earth, as it is in heaven"* and *"Whatsoever ye shall bind...loose on earth shall be bound...loosed in heaven."* The will of God must be authoritatively asked for on earth *before* Heaven will act to have that will accomplished on the earth. Basically, God needs a yielded vessel on the earth who He can work through:

> *For the eyes of the Lord run to and fro throughout the whole earth, to* **shew himself strong in the behalf of them whose heart is perfect toward him**. *Herein thou hast done foolishly: therefore from henceforth thou shalt have wars* (2 Chron. 16:9)

God searches for someone *on the earth* to display His strength on their behalf. By covenant right, God cannot just do anything that He wants on the earth. As far as power and ability are concerned, God certainly could do what He wants. However, God is a God that keeps covenant and in His integrity He will never use His power in a way that breaks covenant.

Once God gave man this authority He respected it. Man became responsible for inviting God into the earth to intervene on his behalf. Quite often, men fail to pray and ask God to display His power and this is why we seldom see it. Hence God's eyes go to and fro throughout the earth looking for someone to invite Him in to intervene.

Again this answers the age old question that if "God is all good and all powerful, why does evil exist? Why doesn't He do something about it?" Evil exists because a good and all powerful God respected the covenant that He made with mankind despite the great pain He endures when He sees what we do with that covenant freedom.

Nevertheless, this passage shows us the love of God in how He uses His power on our behalf. He is searching for people that He can help. Satan, on the other hand, is looking for people to use the power he has usurped so that he can devour them (1 Pet. 5:8-9). In other words, while God wants to *use* His great power to help and bless, Satan wants to *abuse* the little power that he has to steal, kill, and destroy (John 10:10). Let us learn to yield to an omnipotent God who desires to show Himself strong on our behalf.

Lack of Prayer and the Rise of Evil

The rise and increase of evil in the earth is not God's fault but the fault of His covenant people. He has depended on us to pray so that He can intervene. Yet, we keep waiting for God to do something about the evil. We sing our hymns, preach our sermons, and wait on Jesus to come back and rid this world of Satan. While the day is coming when Jesus will rid this world of evil forever, He is waiting for His people to cooperate with Him in doing something about it right now.

Why do we have a lack of God's intervention? James says, *".... yet ye have not, because ye ask not"* (James 4:2). The only way to receive is by asking:

> *Ask, and it shall be given you.... For every one that **asketh** receiveth.... how much more shall your Father which is in heaven*

give good things to them that ask him? (Matt. 7:7, 8, 11)

If we want it then we must ask for it. If we do not have it then it is due to our failure to ask. There are many things that God desires to do but our failure to ask has prevented Him. Asking is the law of the kingdom if we expect to receive anything from God (Psalm 2:7-8; Matt. 21:22; John 15:16; 16:23-24; James 1:5; 1 John 5:16).

Hannah, who was childless was finally able to receive, *"....Because I have asked him of the LORD"* (1 Sam. 1:20b). Hannah asked from the Lord and God healed her and gave her the ability to have children. This was *because* she *asked*. The *asking* was the *cause* of her conceiving. Hannah credits her ability to have children to the fact that she asked of God. The reason that God gives is *because* we ask. The reason He is unable to give is *because* we do *not* ask.

It may be God's perfect will to give us a thing but we will never receive it apart from our asking. Ezekiel explains:

> *Then the heathen that are left round about you shall know that I the LORD build the ruined places, and plant that that was desolate: I the LORD have spoken it, and I will do it. Thus saith the Lord GOD;* ***I will yet for this be enquired of by the house of Israel, to do it for them****; I will increase them with men like a flock* (Ezek. 36:36-37)

The "I wills" in this passage is a clear indication of "God's will." There is no mysterious sovereign will of God here. God always reveals His will through His Word and through the Holy Spirit speaking to us. God is more than willing to give Israel an increase in men but it will not happen apart from their asking for it. If Israel has not increased with men like a flock it is due to their failure to enquire of Him to do it.

What Happens when we Don't Pray

This principle holds true for anything that we need God to do on the earth. If we need God to intervene and deal with evil on the earth then God's people must come together, pray with confidence and authority and get this done. Many things that God desires to do is not getting done because God's people are not praying and asking. In Ezekiel God says that He must allow destruction to come upon the land because no one asked Him to intervene:

> *And I sought for a man among them, that should make up the hedge, and stand in the gap before me for the land,* **that I should not destroy it***: but I found none. Therefore have I poured out mine indignation upon them; I have consumed them with the fire of my wrath*: **their own way have I recompensed upon their heads***, saith the Lord GOD* (Ezekiel 22:30-31)

What a sad passage of Scripture. God has no desire to punish Israel for their sins despite how much they deserve it. Yet, unless someone stands in the gap He is left with no choice but to allow the fire of His wrath to consume them.

If God does not want to punish why does He *need* someone to tell Him *not* to do it? Can He not just withhold the punishment? When we understand the free-will covenant that God has established with men and His method of punishing, this should remove the confusion.

While the passage tells us that God will personally destroy the land unless asked not to do so, keep in mind the Eastern idiom of permission we studied in a previous chapter in which God is said to do that which He merely permits. God says that He will destroy in the sense that He will remove His hand of protection on Israel and allow the consequences of their rebellion to come upon their heads. God's method of destruction is by *permission* rather than *causation*. This is affirmed by Hosea:

> ***How shall I give thee up, Ephraim? how shall I deliver thee, Israel?*** *how shall I make thee as Admah? how shall I set thee as Zeboim? mine heart is turned within me, my repentings are kindled together. I will not execute the fierceness of mine anger,* ***I will not return to destroy Ephraim:*** *for I am God, and not man; the Holy One in the midst of thee: and I will not enter into the city* (Hosea 11:8-9)

God's method of destroying is to *depart* from the unrepentant sinner or sinning nation, thus removing His protective presence, and allowing the automatic choices of the sinner or nation to take effect (Exodus 12:12, 13, 23; 2 Kings 13:23; 2 Chron. 12:7; Job 2:3-7; Psalm 5:10; 73:27-28; Isa. 34:2; Jer. 7:29-31; 18:7-10; Eze. 21:31; 22:30-31; 32:12-13; Hosea 4:5-6; 11:8-9). Therefore, God needs someone to stand in the gap and ask Him to stay and intervene as Moses did for Israel (Psalm 106:23; Exodus 32:7-14; Deut. 9:18-20).

Why doesn't God intervene? Because His people fail to ask Him to. God said that it was due to Israel's failure to open their mouths wide (a symbol of prayer) that He was unable to fill it and turn their difficult situations around (Psalm 81:10-16). It was because

Joash's failure to strike the ground with his arrows a sufficient number of times that his victory over his enemies were limited (2 Kings 13:14-19). It was Asa's failure to seek the Lord that caused Him to die from a foot disease (2 Chron. 16:12, 13). It was Israel's failure to look to the Lord for help that brought them shame (Isa. 30:1-3; Isa. 31:1, 2). It was the Israelite pastors failure to seek the Lord that hindered their prosperity and caused the sheep to scatter (Jer. 10:21). It was Peter's failure to pray that caused him to fall into the sin of denying our Lord (Luke 22:31-34; Matthew 26:40, 41, 43, 69-75). It was because Joshua and the elders failed to ask for God's guidance that they were deceived into making a covenant with the burdensome Gibeonites (Josh. 9:13-15).

    We are mistaken when we believe that God will intervene when we do not ask Him to do so. God needs His people to pray. Our lack of praying hinders God from working in the earth to deal with the dark forces of evil and intervene on our behalf. Let us start praying fervently for God's intervention if we want to see a decrease in evil upon the earth.

Chapter Ten

Why So Much Warfare and Bloodshed?

The kings came and fought, then fought the kings of Canaan in Taanach by the waters of Megiddo; they took no gain of money. They fought from heaven; **the stars in their courses fought against Sisera** (Judges 5:19-20)

Why do we find so much warfare and bloodshed in the Old Testament? Even more, why did God command so much of it? Many people are troubled by the numerous references to war in the Old Testament. Some are most troubled by the fact that God even commanded the Israelites to fight. Atheists use the Old Testament Biblical "holy wars" to paint a false picture of a cruel deity that they can hate and excuse themselves from worshipping.

However, many sincere Christians are also troubled by all of the physical violence in the Old Testament. They have a difficult time reconciling this with the picture of God given to us by our Lord and Savior, Jesus the Messiah, in the New Testament.

Heavenly Warfare on Earth

Many things that trouble God's people can be resolved when they understand that there is an ongoing spiritual battle in the Heavenlies that has spilled over into our world (2 Kings 6:15-17; Eph. 6:10-13). The "stars" that Deborah is singing about in the opening passage is speaking about angelic beings both good and evil (Job 38:7; Rev. 1:16, 20; 12:3-4, 7-9).

When the king of Assyria threatened Israel and blasphemed God, King Hezekiah and the prophet Isaiah cried out to God. God sent an angel to deal with the situation (2 Chron. 32:20-22; Isa. 37:33-36). We see from this that a *physical* problem was dealt with through *spiritual* means, which proves that the root of the problem in the first place is *spiritual*.

During the time in which the Old Testament was written, many things were resolved by physical warfare. However, much of the warfare we find in the Old Testament is symbolic of the ongoing war between satanic forces of evil and God's forces of good. It was Satan who was behind the evil kings in the Old Testament who threatened Israel (Job 1:12, 14, 15; Isa. 14:4-17; Eze. 28:12-19; Luke 4:5-8; John 8:44; 12:31; 14:30; 16:11; 2 Cor. 4:4; 1 John 5:18-19; Rev. 20:1-8).

Satan is the one who deceives nations (Rev. 20:3, 8). It was Satan who often sought to destroy Israel since it was through this nation from which the Messiah would come to render him his ultimate defeat and free the rest of the world that is under his control. Even today Satan is behind the Islamic terrorist attacks and wars in the Middle East.

Just like Biblical times, these battles are not simply just a bunch of angry nations that can't get along. Diplomacy will not work against demons. Whether we like it or not, we are involved in this war. We must keep our armor on and use it (Eph. 6:10-18).

Pagan Nations and Demonic Worship
Moses exposed the fact that the gods of the other nations were satanic beings when he wrote the following:

> *"**They sacrificed unto devils**, not to God; **to gods** whom they knew not, **to new gods** that came newly up, whom your fathers feared not"* (Deut. 32:17; see also Lev. 17:7; 2 Chron. 11:15; Psalm 106:35-38; 1 Cor. 10:20-21; Rev. 9:20)

The people during this time were not as ignorant of spiritual realities as many of us might be led to believe. Many recent studies concerning historical documents from the Ancient Near East have taught us that the nations during those times strongly believed in a spiritual warfare scenario in which the victory over evil was determined in the spirit realm.

A thorough study of both the Ancient Near East texts and the Bible itself tells us that the kings during these times were commanded by their "god" to go to war against certain nations. They relied heavily upon their deity to help them win these wars. These kings were the human or earthly representation of their nation's deity.

These "gods" instigated wars against Israel and each other because Satan is the true source and originator of violence (Ezekiel 28:14-16; John 8:44). It is Satan that moves men to kill each other and he is the one behind the nations that oppressed Israel during Old Testament times. While God abhors violence He is not a wimpy God that can just let violent beings go about their merry way destroying things. God wars to protect and defend the subjects of His Kingdom. But He does not do this alone. He enlists our help.

When the Israelites served God then they had protection and peace because God kept the Satan-controlled forces at bay. When the Israelites backslid and began to worship the gods of the other nations, not realizing that by doing this that they were worshipping Satan and fallen angels, God allowed them to have their way (Psalm 81:10-16).

While most of us do not engage in the type of fighting that Israel had to do, we must learn from the Old Testament how warfare in the spirit realm is conducted. I am sure that this will not resolve all of our troubled tensions with Old Testament holy war, but it will lessen these tensions by a great degree if we begin to see that these were not only physical wars but a "spill over" from the cosmic warfare taking place in the heavenly realms between God's forces and those of Satan.

The Spread of Abominations

While people in our day do not understand the full and destructive impact of sin, God has done all that He can to convey this message to us. Sin has a negative impact not only upon the person committing the sin but also upon the land that it is being committed:

> *Ye shall therefore keep my statutes and my judgments, and shall not commit any of these abominations; neither any of your own nation, nor any stranger that sojourneth among you: (For all these abominations have the men of the land done, which were before you, and the land is defiled;)* (Lev. 18:26-27)

Read through Leviticus 18 and take note of the sins being committed by the nations that God was going to dispossess. It was not only the blatant worship of false gods that posed a problem but the horrendous acts that they led to them. There were sexual perversions such as incest, bestiality, and homosexuality. People in our generation have been made these acceptable practices for the majority of the world and therefore look upon God as being too stringent in condemning them. However, these practices lead to outbreaks of all kinds of diseases and other epidemics.

Even more, there was the devaluation of human dignity and human life. Children were sacrificed in torturous ways in order to appease their local deities. Even those in our day who don't seem to have any difficulty with the legal slaughter of innocent unborn children might balk at roasting an infant alive in a fire. Nonetheless, if these nations were to continue to exist it would only be a matter of a few centuries that these acts could bring destruction to all of mankind. This is exactly what Satan has been planning in His war against God and humanity.

Sadly people don't get it and reject these Old Testament truths and the necessity for these "holy wars." Modern day people have been desensitized to the horror of sin and its results. Liberal ideology proclaims the false idea that what one person does for pleasure has no effect on others or on society as a whole has impacted how we view God's standards and His methods for dealing with them. Furthermore, pacifist ideas have crept into much of our thinking about God in which we could never see Him using violent means for handling a situation (due to false interpretations of Jesus' explanations of God's laws).

However, God tells the Israelites that the very land was defiled due to these sins. Like any plague, if God were to allow it to spread it could only mean the destruction of the earth as a whole. It was incumbent upon God as the judge of all the earth to deal with the spread of sin in the world.

However, there is a practical lesson for us as well. Are we allowing sin to dwell in our hearts? If we are we must deal with it and ask God to remove it before it completely defiles us and we are destroyed by it.

Why God Commanded Bloodshed

But the question remains as to why God commanded Israel to destroy these nations? Couldn't He have just left them alone to the worship of their false gods and let them destroy themselves? Why all of the bloodshed? When we see how the pagan worship of these nations caused harm to innocent children then we get a better understanding about God's motives. Furthermore, when we see how Israel's failure to destroy these nations allowed them to become influenced by such evil and allowed this evil to spread throughout their own nation then we fully understand why God commended this destruction:

> **They did not destroy the nations, concerning whom the LORD commanded them**: But were mingled among the heathen, and learned their works. And they served their idols: which were a snare unto them. **Yea, they sacrificed their sons and their daughters unto devils**, And shed innocent blood, even the blood of their sons and of their daughters, whom they sacrificed unto the idols of Canaan: and the land was polluted with blood. Thus were they defiled with their own works, and went a whoring with their own inventions. (Psalm 106:34-39)

Many atheists and others opposed to Christianity often cite Old Testament "holy wars" as an example of why they could never serve the God of the Bible. They feel that God often sent Israel on missions to kill, plunder, and destroy for no valid or justifiable reason. Sadly, God's commands to invade and destroy nations have even perplexed genuine Christians, thus moving them to reject the Old Testament as being a relevant document for God's people today.

Very few atheists are willing to take the time to understand the true reasons behind God's actions in the Old Testament. But for the born again Christian, it is the wrong attitude to reject any portion of God's Word. The New Testament itself teaches us that the Old Testament is for doctrine, correction, and encouragement (2 Tim. 3:16; 1 Cor. 10:6; Rom. 15:4).

Several questions are answered in Psalm 106:34-39 concerning why God commanded these nations to be destroyed. One of them has to do with the unseen spiritual warfare that we are all involved in. These nations were serving the devil without repentance and spreading their demonic religion to other nations. Their religion caused such depravity that innocent people were killed, including some of the very children of these worshippers of demons.

It would actually have been more cruel if God had left these nations to continue in the type of wickedness that destroyed innocent lives (just as it would be for Christians to ignore the sin of abortion prevalent in the Western nations today). But even more, sin of this nature spreads like a poison and, as we can see from the psalm above, had its negative influence on godly nations.

God's Mercy Extended to the Nations

Also keep in mind that God is a God of infinite mercy. It took Him a very long time before He finally decided to bring judgment, even for the most horrible of sins, and these pagans certainly committed some horrible sins. God told Abram that He would give these nations four hundred years before judgment came:

> *And he said unto Abram, Know of a surety that thy seed shall be a stranger in a land that is not theirs, and shall serve them; and they shall afflict them four hundred years; And also that nation, whom they shall serve, will I judge: and afterward shall they come out with great substance. And thou shalt go to thy fathers in peace; thou shalt be buried in a good old age. But in*

> the fourth generation they shall come hither again: **for the iniquity of the Amorites is not yet full** (Gen. 15:13-16)

When God told Him His plans concerning Sodom and Gomorrah, a despondent Abraham, concerned about his nephew Lot, responded:

> *That be far from thee to do after this manner, to slay the righteous with the wicked: and that the righteous should be as the wicked, that be far from thee: Shall not the Judge of all the earth do right?* (Gen. 18:25)

God is indeed the judge of all the earth and He will do right. Abraham's problem was not that God would destroy the wicked, but that the righteous would unfairly suffer as well. Today when modern Westerners read about the Israelite conquest of the surrounding nations and the fact that this was all commanded by God, they seem to believe that God was a bloodthirsty tyrant who did wrong by a bunch of nations minding their own business. This simply is not the case. God was not about to destroy a nation full of righteous people.

The surrounding nations were exceedingly wicked. However, the judge of all the earth extended mercy—*four hundred years* of mercy! But sooner or later the wickedness would become full and affect other parts of the earth. This was Satan's plan for world domination.

God extended mercy in order to give them a chance to come into the true knowledge of God. They had Abraham, Melchizedek, and others who proclaimed the true God to them. There was no reason to remain steeped in satanic worship and all of the selfish destruction of their fellow men that came with it. If God did not eventually judge their wickedness then the judge of all the earth would have done wrong.

God is indeed a judge, but a very merciful One. He gave these nations more than enough time to repent. *They got worse.* God was left with no choice but to judge them. Israel would be His instrument.

What about the Women and Children?

One of the most difficult things to understand for all of us is God's command to kill women and children during war (Deuteronomy 2:34; 3:6; Joshua 6:21; 8:25; 1 Sam. 15:3). God said:

> *But of the cities of these people, which the Lord thy God doth give thee for an inheritance, thou shalt **save alive nothing that breatheth** ....That they teach you not to do after all their abominations, which they have done unto their gods; so should ye sin against the Lord your God* (Deut. 20:16, 18).

Some explanations such as "God is sovereign so He can do as He pleases," or "God's standard of holiness is higher than ours" may be true but they do not solve the problem. A sovereign God who also claims to be love would not have such a difficult command recorded in the Bible without a reasonable explanation. God does not dismiss sincere seekers with an attitude that says, "I am the boss so I do whatever I want. How dare you question me?"

Keep in mind that these nations were completely demonized. The demonic infection effected every single being and object to include men, women, children, beast, and property. Jesus had not yet come and defeated Satan so the Israelite could not engage in deliverance ministry.

Failure to utterly destroy everything associated with these nations and their demons would open a door for Satan to bring the same infection to their nation, which is proven to be true time and time again throughout Israel's history.

Israel had no defense against demonic power at the time except to destroy the people and objects in which the demons dwelt. Sadly, this not only included adult men and women, but beasts, babies and inanimate objects as well (Joshua 7:1-26).

After Jesus conquered Satan in the wilderness He returned in the power of the Spirit and brought deliverance to the captives held by Satan's power (Matt. 4:23-24; Luke 4:1-18). Rather than having to command the slaughter of Canaanite children, Jesus was able to *legally* deliver them from the demonic forces that manifested through them (Matt. 15:21-28).

God's people have been commissioned to bring supernatural healing and deliverance to those who have been bound by the false gods of heathen nations (Mark 16:15-20). God's people in the Old Testament only had one option to stay free from demonic principalities which was to slaughter its hosts. Today, because of Christ's work through His death, burial and resurrection, we have the authority to deal with the demons themselves (Luke 10:17-20).

God's Original Nonviolent Plan for the Heathen
One other thing we need to point out in all of this is the fact that bloodshed and war was probably not God's original plan for dealing with these pagan nations:

> *I will send my fear before thee, and will destroy all the people to whom thou shalt come, and I will make all thine enemies turn their backs unto thee. And I will send hornets before thee, which shall drive out*

the Hivite, the Canaanite, and the Hittite, from before thee (Exodus 23:27-28)

While we do not accept extreme pacifist ideas, we should recognize that God is a warrior by *necessity* and not by *desire*. God is at war because Satan and his followers have declared war on God and mankind. God is at war on our behalf. Though God is not a "pacifist," He does abhor violence and killing. He does all that He is able to do to prevent it. A statement that God once made to King David tells us that He does not like His reputation being associated with blatant bloodshed (1 Kings 5:3; 1 Chron. 28:2-3).

In His initial plan concerning the Israelites possessing the land, God appeared to have introduced a method by which there would have been no fighting or bloodshed on Israel's part. He would have simply sent fear and hornets to drive the inhabitants out of the land and allow Israel to take possession (Joshua 2:9-11; 6:1).

Man's actions have a tendency to change God's plans and methods. For example, God never originally wanted to send spies into the land of Canaan. He wanted the people to trust His Word. But the Israelites asked for it to be done (Deut. 1:22-25), so God gave in to their request and commanded that it be done (Num. 13:1-3).

The sad results of this particular act changed another one of God's plans. Ten of the twelve spies came back with an evil report (a report of unbelief that contradicted God's promises). The people believed it, cried all night, and then threatened to kill Aaron and Moses. Whereas God was going to send them into the land immediately, He now changed the plan to wait forty years for the first generation of unbelieving Israelites to die off.

So what brought the change to where God commanded *Israel* to fight instead of Him sending hornets to drive away the inhabitants of the land? Scripture never seems to say. Whatever the reason for the change of plans, the evidence from the passages cited above would indicate that it probably had something to do with Israel's behavior.

As Christians, we should remember that the weapons of our warfare are not carnal, but mighty through God for dealing with spiritual enemies (2 Cor. 10:4-5; Eph. 6:10-18). God's preferred way for us to solve our problems is to let Him fight for us.

Chapter Eleven

Why Did Jesus have to Die for Our Sins?

He that committeth sin is of the devil; for the devil sinneth from the beginning. For this purpose the Son of God was manifested, that he might destroy **the works of the devil** (1 John 3:8)

John sums up the answer to the question that opens this chapter, "Why did Jesus have to die for our sins." Quite often the death, burial, and resurrection of Christ is taught from the perspective that Christ came to appease an angry and wrathful "Father".[1] Oh what a sad, deceptive and distorted picture this is of our Heavenly Father. It was out of sheer unselfish love that the Father sent Jesus to redeem us (John 3:16; Rom. 5:8; 1 John 4:14-19; Rev. 1:5).

Adam's sin brought all of man under bondage to Satan's tyrannical reign. It is due to this tyranny that evil and wickedness runs rampant in this world. Rather than just leave us captive to His enemy, God set out to rescue us. Therefore the redemptive work and salvation message of Jesus is all about His desire to remove man from the problem that man brought upon himself when he sold himself to the devil's slave market.

The Greek word for *"destroy"* in this passage means *"to loose, dissolve, sever, break, demolish."* (Vines).[2] Basically the word *"destroy"* can be understood to mean *"render powerless."*[3] Sin has placed men and women under Satan's dominion and gave him the legal right to attack and hurt us (Acts 26:18; Eph. 2:1-6; 1 John 5:17-20). Jesus came to redeem us from the *works* that the devil legally used to destroy mankind. Our Lord came for the express purpose of destroying Satan's works against us. Jesus now possesses all authority over death (Rev. 1:18) and He is the Word of Life (1 John 1:1).

Was Redemption Planned Before Creation?

Before we delve further into why Jesus, the second member of the eternal Triune Godhead, had to become a man, suffer and die for our sins in order to free us from the evil of this world, we must tackle what I believe is the erroneous idea that God had always planned [for] the fall of His creation and had planned from eternity past that Jesus would go through all of this for our redemption.

The majority of theologians, no matter what theological persuasion they hold to, tell us that God planned redemption *before* He created because He foreknew the fall of man. They believe that God looked through the corridors of time, saw the fall of man, made a covenant with the second member of the Triune Godhead to die for them, and went on ahead and created.

However, as we explained in chapter 8, if God knew beyond a shadow of a doubt that Adam and Eve would fall and plunge us into this catastrophe then He is fully culpable for the evil that is in the world. Furthermore, God, just before the flood of Noah, begins to grieve over man's sin, is very heartbroken, and regrets that He ever created them (Gen. 6:5-7).

None of this makes sense at all if God exhaustively knew that man would fall and that Jesus would be slain for it. Yet, whenever I have publically challenged this idea I have been told that "some things just remain a mystery." Once again when traditional teachings that cause one to question God's goodness in the face of evil are challenged, one can only appeal to "mystery".

Nonetheless, God has given us a book to which He has revealed many of these "mysteries." While God may have hidden some things He does expect us to do the research necessary to get the answers. Solomon said, *"It is the glory of God to conceal a thing: but the honour of kings is to search out a matter"* (Prov. 25:2). The appeal to "mystery" is nothing but a lazy excuse to hold on to centuries old traditional teaching that conflicts with the revealed goodness of God. These "mysteries" continue to exacerbate the so-called "problem of evil."

I don't think people realize how selfish, arrogant, and egotistical these ideas make God out to be. To pre-plan a world that he knew beyond a shadow of a doubt would be plunged into sin, causing billions to suffer eternal damnation, to pre-plan His own death before any of this even happened knowing that only a small minority of sinners would accept Him as Lord and live for Him, and then to tell us, "I am God, I do as I wish, your finite mind can never grasp my reasons for these mysteries" really is not a picture of a loving God at all, especially not the God as revealed in Jesus Christ who explained the mysteries of His parables to those who sought further understanding.

The Foundations of the World

A number of passages are used by theologians to support the premise that God knew that angels and men would fall and planned redemption before He ever created. One of them is found in the book of Revelation:

> *And all that dwell upon the earth shall worship him, whose names are not written in the book of life of* **the Lamb slain from the foundation of the world**. (Rev. 13:8)

The word for "foundation" in the Greek is *katabolē*. The majority of English translations translate the word as "foundation". However, this is not the best translation of *katabolē*. The Harper Collins dictionary says that the root meaning is a "destructive metabolism". W. E. Vine, while acknowledging its use in Scripture, says that *katabole* literally means, "a casting down." Some literal Bible translations recognize the true meaning of *katabole*: *"And all who are dwelling on the earth will be worshiping it, everyone whose name is not written in the scroll of life of the Lambkin slain from **the disruption of the world**"* (Rev. 13:8; Concordant Literal Version).

While some believe that this "disruption of the world" occurred during the gap between Genesis 1:1 and 1:2 (see chapter 1 for a further explanation of the Genesis 1:1-2 gap), I believe that Rev. 13:8 is connected to Genesis 3:15. It was when man sinned, brought a curse on God's good creation, thus disrupting the world, is when God decided that Jesus would die on his behalf. In this respect Jesus was slain *from the disruption of the world*, or when sin brought death into the world (Rom. 5:12).

Some have also appealed to Ephesians 1:4 to support their premise that God not only planned redemption before He created, but *elected* who would be saved and lost before the creation process ever began:

> *According as he hath chosen us in him **before the foundation of the world**, that we should be holy and without blame before him in love.*

The misinterpretation of this passage has led to what I strongly believe is a false teaching that God chose select individuals for salvation before ever creating the world. Some believe, based on the misunderstanding of this passage, that God had specifically created some for salvation and others for damnation. Others claim that God, before He created, looked down the corridors of time, foresaw who would have faith and who would not, elected those that He foresaw would believe in Jesus.

Again, the Concordant Literal Translation is helpful here: *"according as He chooses us **in Him** before the disruption of the world, we to be holy and flawless in His sight."* The "in Him" phrase is the key to this passage. We are chosen through our **union in Christ**. The passage is telling us that God had already chosen everyone *in Christ* before there was ever a disruption due to sin entering the world. We were created by Christ and for Christ and it is by Him that all things consist:

> *For by him were all things created, that are in heaven, and that are in earth, visible and invisible, whether they be thrones, or dominions, or principalities, or powers: all things were created by him, **and for him**: And he is before all things, and **by him all things consist*** (Col. 1:16-17)

Verse 17 in the Concordant Literal Translation says, *"and He is before all, and all has its cohesion **in Him**"* or as the World English Bible says, *"....in him all things are held together."* The reason for the creation of everything was by and for Christ. Therefore we were always chosen *in Him* for Him. The Elders cried, *"....for thou hast created all things, and for thy pleasure they are and were created"* (Rev. 4:11b). Since God never takes pleasure in the death of the wicked then this certainly could not have been a part of His plan (Eze. 18:23, 32, 33:11).

It was the disruption of the world by sin that attempted to sever the loving intentions that God had for man in Christ. However, Christ would not allow this disruption to destroy His eternal intentions. So He became a man to render the ultimate sacrifice. Christ is the *Chosen One* (Matt. 12:18; Luke 9:35). Those who embrace covenant union in Christ become one with Him and are part of the corporate elect.

Jesus died for every single human being in the world and offers this "corporate election" to all (John 3:16-17; 1 Tim. 2:4-6; Tit 2:11; Heb. 2:9; 2 Pet. 3:9; 1 John 2:2). Individual faith in the finished work of Christ brings us into this election (Eph. 1:13; 2:8; 3:17; Acts 20:21; Rom. 1:16; 4:16; 10:9-10, 13 1 Cor. 12:13) and into the plan that God always had before sin disrupted it.

There are other Scriptures used to support the claim that God foresaw the fall of men and angels before He created and planned redemption beforehand. Tackling all of these would take more space than we intend to commit to this subject in this book, but it will not hurt to look at just one more. In Titus 1:2 we find the phrase, *"In hope of eternal life, which God, that cannot lie, promised before the world began."* If what some imply from this translation is true then exactly who did He promise eternal life to? It could not have been any of us since we did not exist before the world began.

While a translation might be accurate, theological bias can often color how it is rendered in English. If one holds to the "God outside of time" theory then their translation, though accurate and literal, will be rendered according to that bias. Others can see the actual thought being conveyed in the translation and render it accurately in that sense.

The Greek phrase in Titus 1:2 would have been better rendered *"the hope of eternal life that God promised **long ago"*** (Contemporary English Version). Others render it, *"promised long ages ago"* (New American Standard Bible, Common New Testament), *"promised ages ago"* (Revised Standard Version, Goodspeed, Moffat, Riverside New Testament, Williams New Testament), and *"promised from the most ancient times"* (Noyes New Testament).

The Earth's Destiny in Man's Hands

There is no need to believe from Titus 1:2 that God foresaw or preplanned the fall of man before He ever created. The simple fact of the matter is that Jesus came to rescue us from the tyranny of Satan that man placed himself under through his disobedience. God said:

> *And the LORD God said unto the serpent, Because thou hast done this, thou art cursed above all cattle, and above every beast of the field; upon thy belly shalt thou go, and dust shalt thou eat all the days of thy life: And I will put enmity between thee and the woman, and between thy seed and her seed;* **it shall bruise thy head**, *and thou shalt bruise his heel.* (Gen. 3:14-15)

When man sided with Satan then God decided that he would deal with Satan once and for all by becoming a man Himself and then bruising his head. It was at this point that redemption was announced and planned. Genesis 3:14-15 was the very first prophecy about Jesus coming to earth as a man and His intentions to *legally* conquer Satan on our behalf. The overwhelming love of God could not allow Him to forsake man though He would have been just to do so.

God never intended for man to take sides with His enemy and plunge the world into sin and chaos. God never meant for man to be subjected to anyone but Himself. In the beginning God created man with authority over the rest of His creation:

> *For thou hast made him but* **little lower than God**, *And crownest him with glory and honor. Thou makest him to have*

dominion over the works of thy hands;
Thou hast put all things under his feet:
(Psalm 8:5-6; American Standard Version)

The phrase "under his feet" means that which is placed there is in subjection to *that* person (Eph. 1:22; Heb. 2:8). It is also a phrase that speaks of having conquered an enemy (Josh. 1:3-5; 2; 10:7-25; Sam. 22:38, 39; 1 Kings 5:3; Psalm 18:37, 38; 47:3; 91:13; Isa. 14:25; Lam. 1:15; Mal. 4:3; Luke 10:17-20; Rom. 16:20; 1 Cor. 15:25; Rev. 11:2).

God had given man full authority and ability to conquer. There was no reason for man to have ever become subjected to Satan, thus plunging the whole world into disaster. At this point, the earth's destiny was not dependent upon God but upon the one God delegated His authority to which was Adam. In his wonderful book on prayer, Andrew Murray writes:

> "Man's destiny appears clearly in God's language at creation. It was to *fill*, to *subdue*, and to have *dominion* over the earth and everything in it. These three expressions show us that man was intended, as God's representative, to rule here on the earth. As God's deputy, he was to fill God's place, keeping everything in subjection to Him. It was the will of God that everything should be done through man, i.e., the history of the earth was entirely in his hands."[4]

God did not send Satan in the garden to *conquer* Adam. **God put Adam on the earth to conquer Satan.** Upon man's creation, God had already placed him in a position of victory over any enemies that would attempt to invade his authorized territory, which was the whole earth as well as the sky around it. Seeing that man was given such vast authority and that all things were placed under his feet, then there was no reason for man to fall.

However, since man did fall and fail to complete the mission for which he was created, God, in His massive love, would become a man Himself and rescue man from what he had done to himself.

Once Adam yielded to Satan, as the representative head of all of mankind, he placed the whole race under Satan's tyrannical reign. This was neither God's plan nor desire. In order for mankind to be rescued from Satan's tyranny it needed a new representative—another man. Yet, it needed one who was not subjected to Satan's kingdom and one who the devil had no rights to. Angels could not rightly represent man because man was not created in their image. The only One who could legally represent man and rescue Him would be God since man was created in God's image. However, God had to become a man in order to accomplish this task. Jesus became that representative man and undid all that Adam had done:

> *For since by man came death, by man came also the resurrection of the dead. For as in Adam all die, even so in Christ shall all be made alive.... And so it is written, The first man Adam was made a living soul; the last Adam was made a quickening spirit* (1 Cor. 15:21-22, 45)

God is not in any way responsible for man's fall either through pre-planning of it or foresight of the fall while deciding to create anyway. If this were true then Jesus becoming a man and dying for us could not be sacrificial love as described in Scripture, but a selfish plan to bring Himself glory. Therefore much "orthodox" theology does little more than malign God's character and questions His unselfish love. Orthodoxy often makes Christ's redemptive work on our behalf meaningless.

Why Such a Violent Death?

The Bible says we were *"sold under sin"* (Rom. 7:14). When we sin we have *sold ourselves*. Scripture says that the one who sins becomes a *slave* to it (John 8:34; Rom. 6:16-20). By extension, we have become a slave to the one who is the master of all sinners, Satan (Gen. 4:7; 1 John 3:8-12; Eph. 2:1-2; Acts 26:18). In Adam's case he sold the whole human race (Rom. 5:18-19). We needed to be "bought back" from this slavery:

> *For thus saith the LORD,* **Ye have sold yourselves for nought**; *and ye shall be redeemed without money* (Isa. 52:3)

The Hebrew word "sold" in this passage is often used in relation to someone being sold as a slave (Lev. 25:50; Psalm 105:15). When we sin we sell ourselves as slaves to Satan for nothing. However, God says that He will redeem us without money. This word means "to buy back." This is what Jesus did by shedding His blood:

> *"Giving thanks unto the Father, which has made us meet to be partakers of the* **inheritance of the saints in light***: Who hath delivered us from the* **power of darkness***, and hath translated us into the kingdom of his dear Son. In whom we have* **redemption through His blood***, even the forgiveness of sins."* (Col. 1:12-14)

Kenneth Wuest translates verse 13, *"....who delivered us out of the tyrannical rule of the darkness and transferred us into the kingdom of the Son of His love."* We were under Satan's tyranny but God "bought us back" by the blood of Jesus and placed us into His kingdom. The blood is more precious than silver or gold (1 Pet. 1:18-19).

Certainly God has the physical power and might to redeem us from Satan by force. However, because God is fair, even to Satan, our redemption would have to be, *"Not by might, nor by power, but by my spirit, saith the LORD of hosts"* (Zec. 4:6). Since man sold himself under Satan God would have to redeem him without force.

The only *righteous* way for God to "buy back" mankind would have to be done *legally,* or, within the keeping of His own righteous laws and standards. Otherwise, God would be accused of holding a double-standard and He could never be trusted in a true sense of what it means to genuinely love and trust someone. Therefore, rescuing mankind from satanic tyranny required the ultimate sacrifice and demonstration of love. This would require God becoming one of these creatures and then dying for them. That is exactly what Christ did through the shedding of His blood:

> *Now is come salvation, and strength, and the kingdom of our God, and the power of his Christ: for the accuser of our brethren is cast down, which accused them before our God day and night.* ***And they overcame him by the blood of the Lamb****, and by the word of their testimony; and they loved not their lives unto the death* (Rev. 12:10-11).

Hebrews 9:22b tells us that, *"....without shedding of blood is no remission."* The only way that this remission could be accomplished is through the innocent blood of another man. Every other human's blood is tainted due to having received Adam's DNA. That is why God Himself had to come. Jesus never sinned so He could say, *"For this is my blood of the new testament, which is shed for many for the remission of sins"* (Matt. 26:28).

It is not your fault that you were born into this sin-filled world. It is not your fault that you inherited Adam's DNA. Nor is it your fault for being born in Satan's prison camp. You are no more at fault for these things than for having caught a virus that is spreading throughout the region you live in. However, if a doctor offers you a vaccine that will cure the virus and you refuse it then you are at fault for rejecting the remedy and will pay the penalty. You are not at fault for inheriting Adam's DNA but you at fault if you reject the solution to the sin-sickness and imprisonment that you were born into.

We have freedom and victory over sin and Satan by the blood of Jesus because His blood gave Satan a crushing defeat. Furthermore, none of it was done *by force* on God's part. **Satan lost his hold on the world when he murdered the innocent Son of God.** On God's part, allowing the shedding of Christ's blood was the legal, nonviolent undoing of Satan's legal reign.

Satan hated God and lusted after the opportunity to kill Him. Satan, like a mad man blinded by hatred, ignored any repercussions that would accrue from killing the sinless, righteous Son of God. He deceived himself into thinking that he could hold God Himself in his prison of death (Acts 2:22-27) and took advantage of the opportunity to kill Him (Luke 22:53). The resurrection of Christ proved him wrong (1 Cor. 15:54-58) because, *"....God raised Jesus and unleashed Him from the agonizing birth pangs of death, for death could not possibly keep Jesus in its power"* (Acts 2:24; The Voice).

The reason that it was not possible for death to keep Jesus in its power is because the wages of *sin* is death (Rom. 6:23; James 1:15). Since Jesus had never sinned Satan blindly and *illegally* placed Jesus under his power of death, thereby forfeiting his legal rights over the earth and mankind.

Chapter Twelve

Why Must Sinners Suffer in Hell?

*Then shall he say also unto them on the left hand, Depart from me, ye cursed, into **everlasting fire, prepared for the devil and his angels*** (Matt. 25:41)

Why is there a hell? Why is it eternal (Mark 3:28-29; Jude 7)? Why must people suffer eternally in hell for a small lifetime of sin on earth?

Punishment Prepared for Satan

Technically speaking, people will first go to hell, later they will stand before the white throne judgment, and afterwards they will be sent to the lake of fire where they will be tormented forever and ever along with Satan and his demons (Rev. 14:9-11; 20:13-14). While we will primarily refer to final punishment as "hell" it is a very important to note these distinctions.

The answers to just about every "why" question concerning evil finds its answer in the rebellion of Lucifer (Latin for "light bearer"), the beautiful angel that God created who, of his own volition, became a "Satan" (accuser) and a "devil" (slanderer). In Isaiah 14 we read:

> ***How art thou fallen from heaven, O Lucifer, son of the morning!*** *how art thou cut down to the ground, which didst weaken the nations! For thou hast said in thine heart, I will ascend into heaven, I will exalt my throne above the stars of God: I will sit also upon the mount of the congregation, in the sides of the north: I will ascend above the heights of the*

> *clouds; I will be like the most High.* **Yet thou shalt be brought down to hell, to the sides of the pit.** *They that see thee shall narrowly look upon thee, and consider thee, saying, Is this the man that made the earth to tremble, that did shake kingdoms; That made the world as a wilderness, and destroyed the cities thereof; that opened not the house of his prisoners?* (Isa. 14:12-17)

For Lucifer's wicked ambitions to be exalted he will be rewarded with being debased. Instead of being exalted above the throne of God he will instead be brought down to a place where neither God's throne nor His presence resides. Since Satan wants nothing to do with God then God has allowed a union between Satan and hell before his final judgment.

Hell: an Enemy of God and Man

A proper theodicy about hell begins with the fact that it is no friend of God's nor is He in partnership with hell. Death and Hell are God's ENEMIES. It was Hell that attempted to trap and hold our Lord's spirit before He overpowered it and was risen from the dead:

> *Whom God hath raised up, having loosed the pains of death: because it was not possible that he should be holden of it. For David speaketh concerning him, I foresaw the Lord always before my face, for he is on my right hand, that I should not be moved.... Because thou wilt not leave my soul in hell, neither wilt thou suffer thine Holy One to see corruption.... He seeing this before spake of the resurrection of*

> *Christ, that his soul was not left in hell, neither his flesh did see corruption* (Acts 2:24, 25, 27, 31)

"Death" in verse 25 is the Greek word "Hades" which is translated "hell" in other parts of the Bible. Hell attempted to hold on to and forever imprison Jesus. Hell was *not* the friend of Jesus. Jesus went to war and defeated hell on our behalf. In his word studies Marvin Vincent says, "....it should be rendered snares of death; the figure being that of escape from the snare of a huntsman."[1] A. T. Robertson adds:

> "....but the Hebrew original means 'snares' or 'traps' or 'cords' of death where sheol and death are personified as hunters laying snares for prey ....'Loosing' (lusas) suits better the notion of 'snares' held a prisoner by death"[2]

Other translations show the antagonistic attitude that Hades, Hell (Death) held towards Christ when it thought it had Him trapped. The Common New Testament edition says, *"God raised him up!* **God freed him from death's dreadful grip***, since it was impossible for death to hang on to him"* (Common English Bible) and the Living Bible paraphrases it, *"Then God released him from* **the horrors of death** *and brought him back to life again, for death could not keep this man within its grip."* These are not pictures of forces working along with Christ but enemies who desire to destroy Him.

However, the Lord was freed from Hell's grip and reigns victorious and supreme over both hell and death. Paul writes, *"For he must reign, till he hath put all enemies under his feet. The* **last enemy that shall be destroyed is death***"* (1 Cor. 15:25-26). Again we see that there is no friendship between Christ and death. It is an enemy that He intends to destroy in the very near future.

It is through His death, burial, and resurrection that those connected to Christ can declare the victory over death and hell:

> *So when this corruptible shall have put on incorruption, and this mortal shall have put on immortality, then shall be brought to pass the saying that is written, Death is swallowed up in victory. O death, where is thy sting? O grave, where is thy victory? The sting of death is sin; and the strength of sin is the law. But thanks be to God, which giveth us the victory through our Lord Jesus Christ* (1 Cor. 15:54-57)

Christ did not need to get a victory over something He was working with to help Him punish sinners. On the contrary, Christ saw both death and hell as enemies that He needed to defeat. The word "Grave" should actually be translated "hell" as it is in most English versions. Nonetheless, because of our Lord's victory over death and hell, Jesus now has the authority (keys) over them and has given them to His church (Rev. 1:18).

So God is not working hand in hand with the devil, death, or hell. These are enemies that are opposed to Jesus and His church:

> *And I say also unto thee, That thou art Peter, and upon this rock I will build my church; and the* **gates of hell shall not prevail against it***. And I will give unto thee the keys of the kingdom of heaven: and whatsoever thou shalt bind on earth shall be bound in heaven: and whatsoever thou shalt loose on earth shall be loosed in heaven* (Matt. 16:18-19)

When Jesus said that the gates of Hell will not prevail against His church He meant that they would not be able to overpower or overcome His church. This is what hell is attempting to do to Jesus and His church. Hell is not in partnership with God. Death and hell are enemies of God. Hell is not trying to work *with* Jesus and His church. It is trying to prevail *against* us.

Although Jesus has defeated these enemies, they will continue to war and do what they possibly can to destroy mankind until Jesus rids us of them forever (Rev. 6:8). The day is coming when God will finally rid the universe of these tormentors (Revelation 20:13-14).

God Does not Want Anyone in Hell

Seeing that hell is no friend but an enemy of God then it stands to reason that He has no desire that any man go there. God is the One *"Who will have all men to be saved, and to come unto the knowledge of the truth"* (1 Tim. 2:4). Peter also writes:

> *The Lord is not slack concerning his promise, as some men count slackness; but is longsuffering to us-ward, not willing that any should perish, but that all should come to repentance* (2 Pete. 3:9)

Many people love to preach on the sovereignty of God, claim that He is in control, and that all things happen according to His will. These two passages are a direct contradiction to this false teaching. All things do not happen according to God's will and, frankly speaking, God does not always get what He wants. He wants all men saved. He doesn't want any of them to perish.

Yet men are dying without Christ on an hourly basis and perishing forever. God derives no pleasure from the fact that people die and separate themselves from Him:

> *Have I any pleasure at all that the wicked should die? saith the Lord GOD: and not that he should return from his ways, and live?* (Eze. 18:23)

> *For I have no pleasure in the death of him that dieth, saith the Lord GOD: wherefore turn yourselves, and live ye* (Eze. 18:32)

> *Say unto them, As I live, saith the Lord GOD, I have no pleasure in the death of the wicked; but that the wicked turn from his way and live: turn ye, turn ye from your evil ways; for why will ye die, O house of Israel?* (Ezekiel 33:11)

God uses death and hell synonymously (2 Sam. 226; Psalm 18:5; 116:3; Prov. 5:5; 7:27; Isa. 28:15-18; Hab. 2:5; John 5:24; Rev. 1:18). God takes no pleasure in the fact that anyone goes there. On the contrary God is pleading with men to be reconciled to Him:

> *To wit, that God was in Christ, reconciling the world unto himself, not imputing their trespasses unto them; and hath committed unto us the word of reconciliation. Now then we are ambassadors for Christ, as though God did beseech you by us: we pray you in Christ's stead, be ye reconciled to God* (2 Cor. 5:19-20)

The Contemporary English Version says, *"We were sent to speak for Christ, and* **God is begging you to listen to**

our message. *We speak for Christ and sincerely ask you to make peace with God."* Christ is begging people to be reconciled to Him. That is how badly He wants to save people. He wants no one to go to hell. He weeps bitterly when people make choices that separate themselves from Him (Jer. 9:1; Hosea 11:8; Luke 19:41-44).

This is why I have no choice but to reject the traditional teachings of God's predestination and foreknowledge. Those who embrace a theology that says that God predestined some to hell before they were ever created are not teaching God as He describes Himself in His Word. The God who dies for sinners, who begs people to turn from sin and who weeps over them when they do not repent, could not be the same one who predestines them to hell in the first place.

However, under that same vein I must reject the God of exhaustive future foreknowledge. Did God know before He created man that the majority of them would end up in hell? Most of the church believes that God knew this. While predestination theology makes God into a wicked tormentor, the exhaustive foreknowledge theology unintentionally makes Him negligent.

Furthermore, exhaustive foreknowledge is completely inconsistent with what God has said about Himself (Gen. 6:5-7; Jer. 7:31; 19:5; 32:35). God holds people responsible for knowing what would happen but not doing something about it (Matt. 25:24-30; 1 Sam. 3:11-13; 2:30). Does God hold a double standard? Certainly not!

Why do Sinners go to Hell

So why do people go to hell if hell is actually an enemy of God and He does not want them there? People go to hell because they *choose* to sin (Gen. 2:15-17; Rom. 6:23; James 1:12-14; Prov. 15:24) and they choose to follow Satan (1 John 3:8; John 8:34; Rom. 6:16).

Neither Hell nor the lake of fire was ever meant for any man. This place was *"....prepared for the devil and his angels."* No man was ever supposed to go there. Why do men go there? Men go to that awful place because they have taken on the character of Satan and continue to follow him:

> *And you hath he quickened, who were dead in trespasses and sins; Wherein in time past ye walked according to the course of this world, according to the prince of the power of the air, the spirit that now worketh in the children of disobedience: Among whom also we all had our conversation in times past in the lusts of our flesh, fulfilling the desires of the flesh and of the mind; and were by nature the children of wrath, even as others* (Eph. 2:1-3)

When we sin we are following the one already destined for eternal damnation. This is the *real meaning of predestination.* One chooses their own destiny. Satan's predestination took place only after he rebelled against God. Those who follow Satan follow His destiny. We share the destiny with the one we choose to follow. If we walk according to the prince of the power of the air then we are going to go exactly where he is going. Since Satan and his followers want nothing to do with God then God will allow them their choice.

God cannot arbitrarily deliver people from hell because they make COVENANTS with it (Isa. 28:15, 18). Some have become "children of wrath" and "children of hell" before they ever get there (Matt. 23:15). God is ever trying to draw men to Himself and offer them salvation but most refuse Him (Luke 7:30; John 5:40; Hosea 11:5-7). In his gospel, John explains why this is so:

> *For God sent not his Son into the world to condemn the world; but that the world through him might be saved. He that believeth on him is not condemned: but he that believeth not is condemned already, because he hath not believed in the name of the only begotten Son of God. And this is the condemnation, that light is come into the world, and **men loved darkness rather than light**, because their deeds were evil. For every one that doeth evil hateth the light, neither cometh to the light, lest his deeds should be reproved* (John 3:17-20)

John points out a number of things here. First, God is not the one bringing condemnation upon men. They are already condemned from the fact that they have chosen sin.

Rather than condemnation, Jesus has offered freedom from condemnation by offering them His light. Yet men reject the light because they prefer the darkness. In other words, men prefer Satan over God:

> *To open their eyes, and to turn them from darkness to light, and from the power of Satan unto God, that they may receive forgiveness of sins, and inheritance among them which are sanctified by faith that is in me* (Acts 26:18)

By hating the light we hate God and want nothing to do with Him. By loving the darkness we continue to follow Satan. God does not condemn anyone to hell. We were destined to go there because we chose to follow Satan. However, Jesus came to give us another choice. We choose Him and our destiny changes. We choose against Him and we will continue on the course that we have chosen (Matt. 7:13-14). Hell and the lake of fire was not prepared for any man but still awaits those who follow the one that it was prepared for.

Hell: Reaping what we have Sown

One evening while listening to the radio I heard one of the "God predestines select people to hell" teachers plainly state that God Himself will be in hell torturing the sinners. What an awful picture of God. When we have rejected the provision of Christ and chosen a life of sin, hell pulls the unrepentant sinner down like a gravitational force upon death (Psalm 116:3; Isa. 5:14; Luke 16:22-23). One of my favorite authors, S. D. Gordon, well says:

> In its essence' death is separation from God. All life is the breath of God. Sin is cutting one's self off from God. It is like gripping a man by the throat with tightening clutch until the breath of life departs. Sin is choosing to leave God out. The very act cuts off the source of life. The grammar of the verb to sin is peculiar to itself. It is this: present tense, to sin; first future tense, following instantly on the present, to suffer; in the second future tense the verb changes its form, it becomes a noun—hell. That hateful, ugly word hell, which the lips utter only by compulsion when they must, for the sheer pain of it, is simply the name given to the place where death reigns; where God has been excluded. They who prefer to leave God out will gather together at some time ***by a natural moral affinity, or gravitation***. The name used for such meeting-place in this old Book is that hurting word hell. Hell- is death's abode. God shut out, no life, death, death regnant—that is hell.[3] (Emphasis are mine)

God says that hell is the result of sinners having sunk in the pit of their own making and being snared by the works of their own hands:

> *The heathen are sunk down in the pit that they made: in the net which they hid is their own foot taken. The LORD is known by the judgment which he executeth: the wicked is snared in the work of his own hands. Higgaion. Selah.* **The wicked shall be turned into hell**, *and all the nations that forget God* (Psalm 9:15-17)

God's judgment is to remove whatever protection He has held over them and then allow them to be snared in the work of their own hands. It is the sinner that makes the pit that he eventually sinks down into and it is his own net that he lays for others that catches him. It is the results of their free-will choices that God will finally let them suffer. But what about those passages that teach that God personally destroys sinners in hell. Let's look at one:

> *And fear not them which kill the body, but are not able to kill the soul: but rather fear him which is able to destroy both soul and body in hell.* (Matt. 10:28)

We must take the time to understand exactly how God is said to "destroy". In Matthew 7:13 Jesus tells us that each person who goes to hell does so through their own free-choice: *"Enter ye in at the strait gate: for wide is the gate, and* **broad is the way, that leadeth to destruction,** *and many there be which go in thereat:"* When people make this choice of their own free-will God tells them to *"depart from me"* (Matt. 7:23; 25:41). God destroys people by removing them from His protective presence and "giving them up" and "delivering them" to the results of their choices:

> ***How shall I give thee up, Ephraim? how shall I deliver thee, Israel?*** *how shall I make thee as Admah? how shall I set thee as Zeboim? mine heart is turned within me, my repentings are kindled together. I will not execute the fierceness of mine anger,* ***I will not return to destroy Ephraim:*** *for I am God, and not man; the Holy One in the midst of thee: and I will not enter into the city* (Hosea 11:8-9)

God's method of destroying is to depart from the unrepentant sinner, thus removing His protective presence, and allowing the automatic choices of the sinner to take effect (Exodus 12:12, 13, 23; 2 Kings 13:23; 2 Chron. 12:7; Job 2:3-7; Psalm 5:10; 73:27-28; Isa. 34:2; Jer. 7:29-31; 18:7-10; Eze. 21:31; 22:30-31; 32:12-13; Hosea 4:5-6).

It appears that in Luke's version of this teaching that Jesus is speaking about denying those who deny Him (Luke 12:4-9). In hell, those who wanted nothing to do with God will receive their choice. Sadly, that choice comes with destruction. This is the "sowing and reaping" process at work here. Therefore, God "destroys" by no longer stopping the reaping from taking place (Ps. 9:15-17). The sad part about "reaping" is that the harvest is always bigger than the seed sown.

The greatest horror of hell is that God's presence is not there. Hence merciless eternal torment and destruction will be the result of those who reject Christ.

Chapter Thirteen

Why are Christians Confused about Evil?

> *See, I have set before thee this day life and **good**, and death and **evil**.... I call heaven and earth to record this day against you, that I have set before you life and death, **blessing and cursing**: therefore choose life, that both thou and thy seed may live* (Deut. 30:15, 19)

There are a number of theologians who teach an idea about the sovereignty of God that does not line up with what the common man understands as someone who can be classified as "just" or "good." The type of sovereignty that is taught makes God appear more devilish and contradictory than what is universally understood as "good." When this is brought to the attention of these sovereignty advocates, they rebut with statements such as, "God's ways are higher than our ways" or "God's attributes cannot be scrutinized by human standards" or "We should define goodness by the way God defines it."

I agree with the last statement though the hyper-sovereignty advocates and I would definitely approach it differently. Nonetheless, we will look to Scripture to see how God defines what it means for Him to be *good*.

The Bible Clearly Explains "Good" and "Evil"

In our opening passage God (speaking through Moses) tells His people that He has set before them several things and clarifies them with their synonyms. God says that *life, good,* and *blessings* are synonymous terms and then gives their opposites which are *death, evil,* and *cursing*.

In Deuteronomy 28, which is two chapters before our opening chapter, God listed a number of things that He specifically described as "blessing" and "cursing". God tells us that health in body and mind, prosperity in whatever we do, abundant provision of all needs, victory over our enemies, a good reputation, good weather, lack of debt, and being on top are all *blessings* which means that they are all *good things*. These are the promised results of obedience.

On the other hand, God tells us that disobedience will result in sickness, death, defeat, humiliation, and poverty. God lists a variation of each of these things and this list is very long. Yet, to ensure the listeners that He did not give them an exhaustive list He tells them that there are some sicknesses not even on the list that will come as a result of disobedience (see v. 61).

The Bible makes clear what God considers to be "good and evil" and "blessing and cursing." No need for guessing or philosophical redefinitions of what God might consider as "good". The Bible makes it absolutely clear. Those who want to know how God defines "good" only need to read Deut. 28 and they will no longer be in doubt.

However, the understandable objection is easily raised that God says here that He would personally do the cursing. Indeed in Deuteronomy 28 God makes statements such as, ""I will destroy thee.... I will smite thee.... I will send enemies.... I will send pestilence.... etc." In chapter 6 we looked at why the Bible attributes evil to God and learned that the language being used in this and other passages is merely permissive. I would encourage the reader to go back and read that chapter again (and some of our other material that deals with this subject extensively). We will look at this again momentarily but for now remember that God only dispenses good gifts (Matt. 7:7-11; James 1:17) and is only said to curse (bring evil) when He has removed His protective presence (Joshua 7:11-12; Mal. 3:6-9). It is partly due to the neglect of this Eastern permissive idiom that many theologians and denominational leaders have distorted the truth about what is good and evil and what actually comes from God's hand as a blessing.

Sickness is Evil, Healing is Good

Since many Christians allow their favorite theologian, Bible teacher, or denominational creed to define for them what is good and evil rather than reading the Bible and learning exactly what God has said, they remain confused. Many theologians have blurred the lines between what is good and what is evil and we have been told that certain evils are "blessings in disguise."

God removes this blur in Deuteronomy 28 and elsewhere while telling us exactly what He defines as good. Sickness is one of many examples in which many theologians and denominational leaders have claimed is a good thing from the perspective of God supposedly working in our lives. The Word of God teaches a totally different idea.

In Psalm 107 we read, *"Oh that men would praise the LORD for his goodness, and for his wonderful works to the children of men!"* (v. 15). One of the "wonderful works" that express God's goodness is His healing and deliverance when people cry out to Him:

> *Fools because of their transgression, and because of their iniquities, are afflicted. Their soul abhorreth all manner of meat; and they draw near unto the gates of death. Then they cry unto the LORD in their trouble, and he saveth them out of their distresses. He sent his word, and* **healed them***, and delivered them from their destructions* (Psalm 107:17-20)

God's goodness is demonstrated in bringing healing to men, even after they have done things to bring destruction upon themselves. The destruction that comes upon men is not due to any arbitrary sovereignty of God but due to the iniquity of men. Nevertheless, God's goodness is demonstrated by His willingness to heal. Furthermore, God describes sickness as something that is destructive. There is no good purpose in sickness. In another place we are told that disease is evil:

> *And the LORD will take away from thee all sickness, and will put none of the **evil diseases** of Egypt, which thou knowest, upon thee; but will lay them upon all them that hate thee* (Deut. 7:15)

Diseases are not described as "good" but as "evil". God is not the dispenser of evil things. The word "lay" in this passage is the Hebrew word *"nathan"* and it should be translated either as "permit" or "give them over to".

In Job 2:7 we are told that, *"....went Satan forth ....and smote Job with sore boils from the sole of his foot unto his crown."* Later in Job 42:11 we told that Job's family and friends, *"....comforted him over all the evil that the Lord had brought upon him."* Here we learn two important truths: sickness has its source in Satan which makes it evil in and of itself and that due to the idiomatic expressions of Job's time and culture, God took responsibility for Satan's work. However, Jesus shows us that God is the source of the good only and He dispenses this good to thwart the evil that Satan dispenses:

> *How God anointed Jesus of Nazareth with the Holy Ghost and with power: **who went about doing good, and healing all that***

***were oppressed of the devil**; for God was with him* (Acts 10:38).

God's goodness is demonstrated through the life of Christ. Christ never went about making anyone sick. He went about healing. The Bible defines this as something good. Sickness is defined here as the work of Satan. God was opposing the work of Satan and not using him as some agent to fulfill His "secret and mysterious will." This is consistent with Moses' teaching in Deut. 28 and Deut. 30:15, 19.

Poverty is Evil, Abundance is Good

Like sickness the Bible has nothing positive to say about poverty. Solomon wrote, *"The rich man's wealth is his strong city: the destruction of the poor is their poverty"* (Prov. 10:15). Like sickness, poverty is never a blessing. It actually *destroys* people. In the well-known historical account of Lazarus the beggar who went to Abraham's bosom and the rich man who went into hellish flames, Jesus repeats some words by Abraham that describes the nature of poverty and abundance:

> *But Abraham said, Son, remember that thou in thy lifetime receivedst thy **good things**, and likewise Lazarus **evil things**: but now he is comforted, and thou art in torment* (Luke 16:25)

Note how Abraham defines what is "good" and what is "evil." Abraham never once tells us that Lazarus' poverty was a good thing sent from God. On the contrary, he describes what Lazarus suffered as "evil." The rich man's wealth and abundance was described as a "good thing." Since Jesus related the story He obviously agreed with Abraham's assessment.

The rich man did not go to hell because he was rich. If that was true then Abraham should have been there too because the Bible says that he was VERY RICH (Gen. 13:2). The rich man went to hell because he blatantly disobeyed God's laws. The law said that God's people were not to harden their hearts towards their poor brother or shut their hand from him (Deut. 15:4-11). If Lazarus poverty was a good thing then the rich man should not have gone to hell for keeping Lazarus poor. He should have been rewarded for helping Lazarus stay poor if poverty is good. The truth is poverty, as Abraham correctly said, is evil and wealth is good.

Despite the teachings of ascetic religions, including that of some "Christian" traditions, poverty is never for the purpose of making one more humble and pious as so many claim. Proverbs blames poverty on sin (Prov. 6:10-11; 13:17-18; 20:13; 23:20-21; 28:19). Like sickness, the one who is in poverty may not have personally committed the sin that brought the poverty, but poverty is indeed the result of sin's working.

We must remember that we live in a fallen world where Satan rules. Deprivation, sickness, and lack are the results of mankind allowing himself to be ruled by a malevolent being. When the world allows the evil one to rule it, evil will have its way in its many forms and this includes poverty.

Yet some will rightly argue that the Bible says that God is the One who makes people poor or rich. They have a point. Note Hannah's praise to God:

> *The Lord killeth, and maketh alive: he bringeth down to the grave, and bringeth up.* **The Lord maketh poor, and maketh rich**: *he bringeth low, and lifteth up* (1 Sam. 2:6-7)

In this passage Hannah offers praise to God for opening her womb and allowing her to get pregnant after years of being barren. Some who adhere to "predestination theology" have cited this passage to prove that God is in charge of human destinies. They use this passage to claim that God is the One who determines who will be rich or poor.[1] However, Hannah is making a similar statement to the one that Job made when he lost his wealth. He said:

> *And said, Naked came I out of my mother's womb, and naked shall I return thither:* ***the Lord gave, and the Lord hath taken away;*** *blessed be the name of the Lord. In all this Job sinned not, nor charged God foolishly* (Job 1:21-22)

Yet, when we look at the verses before Job's statement we have no doubt that the person who took away his abundance was not God but Satan. In Job 1:12 we read, *"And the LORD said unto Satan, Behold, all that he hath is in thy power."* It was Satan that stirred up enemies to kill Job's servants and steal his property. It was Satan who used natural disasters to destroy Job's property and kill his children. God did not command Satan to do any of this nor did He have a part in it whatsoever. This was all Satan's doing and done of his own initiative. God's part was only to reluctantly permit Satan to destroy Job (see Job 2:3).

Yet, Job did not sin because he was using the common idiom of his time in which God is said to do that which He merely permits or does not prevent from happening. When we connect Job's crediting of his poverty to Hannah's statement we see that she also was simply worshipping God using the Eastern idiomatic language that was natural to her culture.

God is actually the One who gives us things richly to enjoy (1 Tim. 6:17). However, when we refuse to enjoy what He has generously given and decide to turn from Him then we will suffer poverty. This is called a "curse" and *not* a "blessing" (Deut. 28:47-48). God has established the "sowing and reaping" laws that, when used properly, actually do place our destiny into our own hands (Mal. 3:6-12; Luke 6:37-38; 2 Cor. 9:6-12). Failure to work these laws as God intended leads to poverty (Proverbs 11:23-25). Once God has given us the means by which we can prosper, everything else is left in our hands and we are at fault for not obeying His laws of prosperity.

God's perfect will as seen through Israel is that there would be no poor among them (Deut. 15:4). God's general design was that there be no poor at all. The blessing of God is not *poverty* but *abundance*. However, God is a realist. He knows that not everyone is going to be at the level of the blessing He desired for all of His people. Nonetheless, He did not want those who received the blessing to become hard-hearted towards the poor but to help them (Deut. 15:7). Yet we see that God's will is never poverty but abundance.

Scriptures Misused to Blur the Lines

Sickness and poverty are only two out of many examples in which some have called "evil" good and "good" evil (Isa. 5:20). It seems that anything that most men naturally consider to be evil and that the Bible itself says is the work of Satan such as accidents (Luke 13:3-5), marriage issues (1 Cor. 7:5), natural disasters (Job 1:12, 16, 18-19; Mark 4:37-40), criminal acts to include murder (Job 1:17; John 8:44, 10:10), persecution of God's people (Rev. 2:10; 1 Pet. 5:8-9), unanswered prayer (Daniel 10:12-14), and even sin itself (Gen. 3:1-7; Matt. 4:3; 6:13; 1 Thess. 3:5; 1 John 3:8) is said by some to be good and the work of God.

One of the worse ideas under this teaching is the belief that God may not want to save any of our unsaved family members because He has predestined them to hell. All other types of tragedies can be "good" under this philosophical idea for numerous and supposedly mysterious reasons.

There are also the philosophers and theologians who acknowledge the truth that evil truly is *evil*, but they claim that God either ordains it or permits it for some so-called "greater good". Therefore, in some sense, even though the evil is evil, it is supposedly good because a greater good could not have happened or a worse evil could not have been prevented apart from God ordaining or permitting the evil. If we are to have confidence in prayer then we need to repudiate such false notions by studying the Scriptures.

Too many theologians redefine what is meant by "good" to fit within the parameters of their philosophical views about God. Romans 8:28 is probably the most misused Bible passage in support of these strange ideas of "good" as it pertains to God:

> *Likewise the Spirit also helpeth our infirmities:* ***for we know not what we should pray for as we ought****: but the Spirit itself maketh intercession for us with groanings which cannot be uttered. And he that searcheth the hearts knoweth what is the mind of the Spirit, because* ***he maketh intercession for the saints according to the will of God.*** ***And*** *we know that all things work together for good* ***to them that love God****, to them who are the called according to his purpose.* (Rom. 8:26-28)

The James Moffat Translation renders the passage: *"We know also that those who love God, those who have been called in terms of his purpose, **have his aid and interest in everything**."* Romans 8:28 is teaching us that God comes to supply His *aid* and *interest* in everything. However, He is "a gentleman" and does not force His aid upon us. He requires our *cooperation*. Citing Moffatt's translation in his commentary, C. H. Dodd writes:

> ....the familiar translation is not an admissible rendering of the Greek. Paul did not write: 'All things work together for good to them that love God.' The literal translation is: 'With those who love God, He' (or, according to the other reading, 'God') 'co-operates in all respects for good.' Dr. Moffat has paraphrased this somewhat freely, but with fidelity to the meaning.[2]

It is sad that the devil has used this passage to deceive many Christians into believing that sickness, poverty, tragedy, sin, etc. are from the hand of God. He has deceived many into believing that to "grin and bear these things" and to "thank God for them" is living in victory. A passage that should strengthen confidence in God's aid has been used to cause Christians to proclaim a counterfeit victory with a "bend over and take it" theology.

The victory does not come from calling good evil and evil good or in calling a blessing what God has clearly stated is a curse (Isa. 5:20; Deut. 30:15, 19). The victory comes from appropriating the help of God in resisting all of the evil that comes into our lives.

Meaning "Evil" for "Good"

Genesis 50:20 (often cited in conjunction with Romans 8:28) is another often misused text to teach this philosophical distortion of "good" and "evil":

> *But as for you, ye thought evil against me; but God meant it unto good, to bring to pass, as it is this day, to save much people alive* (Gen. 50:20)

Too often this passage, along with Romans 8:28, is taught in a way that not only contradicts other passages of Scripture, but makes God's character appear to be questionable. This passage is taught in a way that makes it appear as if God is the author of sin. Such an idea would contradict James 1:13-16 which implicitly tells us that God does not tempt men to sin. The sin of Joseph's brothers was the sin of envy, a sin attributed to the flesh and the devil and not to God (Acts 7:9-14; Gal. 5:19-21; 1 John 3:12).

The brothers *thought* evil against Joseph but God specifically declares that His thoughts and ways and the evil thoughts and ways of men are in contrast (Isa. 55:7, 8). Furthermore, God does not endorse the *slanderous* idea that some have taken from this passage that God brings about evil so that good will come out of it (Rom. 3:7-8; see also 6:1-3; James 1:20).

God becomes very weary when we spread false ideas about the nature of His goodness (Mal. 2:17). Therefore, Genesis 50:20 and Romans 8:28 should not be isolated from other Scriptures to teach a twisted idea about how God brings about His plans. We must learn to study passages such as Gen. 50:20 in the light of other portions of Scripture and also in light of *Hebraic idiomatic language*. In his book, **"The Character of God,"** Fergus Ferguson wrote:

> For it is to be recollected by us occidentals, that it is according to the genius of all oriental tongues to ascribe to a powerful individual and par excellence the Divine Being, the doing of that which he only

permits to be done. On the same principle may the divine character be cleared from those clouds that have been drawn over it in connection with the sins of Joseph's brethren, which "he meant unto good" (Gen. 50:20); the hardening of Pharaoh's heart (who is also said to have hardened his own heart); "the Assyrian the rod of God's anger," and the Jews who committed murder at the crucifixion of Christ, and thus carried out God's purpose of love.[3]

Understanding Hebrew idiomatic language would clear up a lot of unnecessary frustration that many people have with the Old Testament and how it appears to contradict the picture that Jesus gives us of God in the New Testament. Hebrew idioms in the Old Testament are often interpreted in a *causative* sense but they should be understood in a *permissive* sense. Understanding this would prevent us from believing that it is necessary to reinterpret the meaning of "good" and evil as it relates to God since many things ascribed to Him in the Old Testament as the cause can be better understood as only being *permitted* due to the free actions of men and devils.

Chapter Fourteen

Why is God Waiting so Long to Destroy Evil?

> *Nevertheless we, according to his promise, look for new heavens and a new earth, **wherein dwelleth righteousness**. Wherefore, beloved, seeing that ye look for such things, be diligent that ye may be found of him in peace, without spot, and blameless. And account that the longsuffering of our Lord is salvation; even as our beloved brother Paul also according to the wisdom given unto him hath written unto you* (2 Pet. 3:13-15)

There is coming a day when this old earth with all of its evil will be done away with and we will have a new universe where only righteousness dwells. Yet, many ask, "Why is God waiting so long to put down evil forever?" It is an understandable question and one we hope to answer to the reader's satisfaction in this final chapter.

The Final Destruction of Evil

In chapter five we spoke about how God, after the 1000 year reign of Christ on the earth, will give mankind one more opportunity to decide between Satan and God. Sadly we see that most will choose Satan over God (Rev. 20:1-8). After this last trial God will rid the universe of Satan, his demonic forces, and sadly, all of the men and women who chose to follow Satan by failing to repent of their wicked deeds:

> *And **the devil that deceived them was cast into the lake of fire and brimstone**, where the beast and the false prophet are, and*

*shall be tormented day and night for ever and ever. And I saw a great white throne, and him that sat on it, from whose face the earth and the heaven fled away; and there was found no place for them. And I saw the dead, small and great, stand before God; and the books were opened: and another book was opened, which is the book of life: and the dead were judged out of those things which were written in the books, according to their works. And the sea gave up the dead which were in it; and death and hell delivered up the dead which were in them: and they were judged every man according to their works. And **death and hell were cast into the lake of fire**. This is the second death. And whosoever was not found written in the book of life was cast into the lake of fire* (Rev. 20:10-15).

Then shall he say also unto them on the left hand, Depart from me, ye cursed, into everlasting fire, prepared for the devil and his angels (Matt. 25:41)

In these passages we see that Satan and every evil force, to include death and hell, will be removed from God's righteous people to a place where they can no longer hurt anyone. Paul said, *"The last enemy that shall be destroyed is death"* (1 Cor. 15:26). Since death is synonymous with evil then we can say that this will be the final destruction of evil (Deut. 30:15, 19).

With Satan, his evil forces, and unrepentant evil-doers out of the way forever the dream of a utopia where there are no more trials, problems, pain or anything harmful becomes a reality. Evil has brought all of the hurt and pain. However, it will no longer be allowed in God's new universe:

> *And there shall in no wise enter into it any thing that defileth, neither whatsoever worketh abomination, or maketh a lie: but they which are written in the Lamb's book of life* (Rev. 21:27)

> *For without are dogs, and sorcerers, and whoremongers, and murderers, and idolaters, and whosoever loveth and maketh a lie* (Rev. 22:15)

These were all the works that Satan swayed men to do (John 8:44; 1 John 5:18-19). All that has been the cause of evil upon this earth will be no more once Satan and his followers have been removed from God's universe and placed in an area where they will be tormented forever and ever as a result of their own evil deeds. Without this evil we will have nothing but peace, joy, and happiness for an eternity.

A Universe Free of Evil

Furthermore, Both Peter and John speak about the creation of a new Heaven and a new Earth (2 Pet. 3:13; Rev. 21:1-2).Herschel H. Hobbs says, "In the beginning God created the heavens and the earth and pronounced them good (Gen. 1). But evil marred that creation. Now John saw a new heaven and a new earth which will never be defiled by evil."[1] God our Father, our Lord Jesus Christ, and the precious Holy Spirit will work together to make all things new. John writes:

> *And I heard a great voice out of heaven saying, Behold,* **the tabernacle of God is**

> *with men, and he will dwell with them, and they shall be his people, and God himself shall be with them, and be their God. And God shall wipe away all tears from their eyes; and there shall be no more death, neither sorrow, nor crying, neither shall there be any more pain: for the former things are passed away* (Rev. 21:3-4)

We have already learned that "death" and "evil" are synonymous (Deut. 30:15, 19). We are promised in God's new universe that *"....there shall be no more death, neither sorrow, nor crying, neither shall there be any more pain."* Since death will be thrown into the lake of fire then all of the sorrow and pain that it causes will be gone with it.

In Christ's new world there is nothing that shall *"hurt nor destroy in all my holy mountain"* (Isa. 11:9).With all of the misery from evil that will be gone at the creation this new heaven and new earth there will be no need to ever cry again. There will only be joy and rejoicing (Isa. 65:17-19). Furthermore the *curse* will be done away with:

> *In the midst of the street of it, and on either side of the river, was there the tree of life, which bare twelve manner of fruits, and yielded her fruit every month: and the leaves of the tree were for the healing of the nations. And* **there shall be no more curse***: but* **the throne of God and of the Lamb shall be in it***; and his servants shall serve him* (Rev. 22:2-3)

Again, the "curse" is synonymous with "death" and "evil" (Deut. 30:15, 19). Note that death and the curse is removed because God and Jesus are in it. The problem of evil does not concern God's presence *but the absence of His presence.* It has been our evil doings that have separated this world from God (Isa. 59:1-2).

Contrary to popular beliefs (and some English translations of the Bible), God did not personally or supernaturally put a curse on the earth. Genesis says:

> *And unto Adam he said, Because thou hast hearkened unto the voice of thy wife, and hast eaten of the tree, of which I commanded thee, saying, Thou shalt not eat of it: cursed is the ground **for thy sake**; in sorrow shalt thou eat of it all the days of thy life* (Gen. 3:17)

"For thy sake" is another way of saying "because of you." The New English Translation says, *"cursed is the ground thanks to you."* This translation definitely puts the onus on Adam for having brought the curse upon the earth. The Wycliffe Translation says, *"the ground shall be cursed on account of thee, **that is, because of thy sin**."* This translation is consistent with Romans 5:12:

> *Wherefore, as by one man sin entered into the world, and **death by sin**; and so death passed upon all men, for that all have sinned*

God did not bring the curse or the resulting death into the world. This was all Adam's doing with help from Satan. The demonstration of God's love is the fact that He stepped into a situation that was not of His own fault or making and will undo the evil that was done upon His creation by us. God did not start this mess but for our sakes He will end it. A. B. Simpson sums it up well:

> The other feature of the renovated earth will be that there will be no sin and nothing that defiles will enter into the holy city and the happy life of the coming ages. Satan will never tempt again. There will be no more curse or cursed one. Never again will God have to cloud His face and perform the strange work of judgment which He so little loves, but the universe will settle down to everlasting love and uninterrupted joy. We will be established and will know that we will never fall again. Angels will be confirmed in their light and holy state and the very shadow of evil will at last be forgotten. Heaven will be so pure that evil will not be a thought, remembered or conceived. The curse of time is to know both good and evil. In the innocence of those happy years man will not know evil but only good. Oh, for that day to come when the crushing, defiling shadow of sin and doubt and fear will never fall again![2]

Imagine no more heartbreak, battles with sickness, fear of the unknown, financial worries, lawsuits, and work that is burdensome, tiresome, and does not appear to achieve anything significant. All of this will be replaced by service to the Lamb that is meaningful and contributes to the joy and happiness of the universe. No more concern about healthcare, aging, insurance and all of the burdensome things in this evil world. Oh how I rejoice in my heart as I write these words right now.

Why the Wait?

Amidst all of the present suffering in this world, what is God waiting for? Children are starving in different parts of the world, governments are oppressing and persecuting God's own people, terrorism is on the rise, wars and rumors of war are increasing, and corruption seems to prevail in every part of our government, our corporations, and even many of our religious institutions and churches.

While all of God's people are so happy that Jesus will one day come and make everything right, many of us, and especially those among us presently suffering terrible trials, keep wondering why God is taking so long to deal with this mess once and for all? We have no doubt that He is going to do it but we want to know *when!*

One reason that God is waiting is due to the fact that He needs time to prove the accusations of Satan that have been launched against Him to be utterly false. Eternity will not be so wonderful and blissful if we enter into it with the false beliefs about God that have been propagated throughout the world and even in many theological circles. For our sakes God needs time to prove that His way of governing is the best way and all of the evil we see around us must be completely understood as Satan's way of governing. When God finally rids the world of evil He wants us to be sure that He is not ridding the world of anything He has done, but is ridding the universe of Satan's work. This covered in more detail in chapters 4 and 5.

This truth also goes hand in hand with another very important reason that God seems to be taking His sweet time getting rid of evil once and for all and it is that He knows that His doing so will mean the destruction of so many that still may be willing to turn away from their sins if given more time. Again Peter writes:

> *The Lord is not slack concerning his promise, as some men count slackness; but is longsuffering to us-ward,* **not willing that any should perish**, *but that all should come to repentance* (2 Pet. 3:9)

God works along with us now in an attempt to minimize evil but one day it will be gone forever. In the meantime God needs us to preach the gospel to every creature and make disciples of all nations so that we can do as much as possible to minimize the damage upon humanity (Matt. 28:18-20; Mark 16:15-20). We must do what we can to turn people from darkness to light, from the power of Satan unto God (Acts 26:18). It is only by the gospel that we are able to rescue lost souls from Satan's blinding power:

> *But if our gospel be hid, it is hid to them that are lost: In whom the god of this world hath blinded the minds of them which believe not,* **lest the light of the glorious gospel of Christ, who is the image of God**, *should shine unto them. For we preach not ourselves, but Christ Jesus the Lord; and ourselves your servants for Jesus' sake. For God, who commanded the light to shine out of darkness, hath shined in our hearts,* **to give the light of the knowledge of the glory of God in the face of Jesus Christ** (2 Cor. 4:3-6)

Other translations of verse 4 are, *"Christ is the one who is* **exactly like God***"* (Easy to Read Version); *"They cannot see the light, which is the good news about our glorious Christ,* **who shows what God is like***"* (Contemporary English Version); *"They cannot see how bright and wonderful Christ is.* **He is just like God himself***"* (World English New Testament).

Our gospel preaching is not to manipulate someone into reciting a "sinner's prayer" in order to claim that we won a soul. Please do not misunderstand me. I fully believe in praying with sinners to receive Christ as

Savior. I am a strong advocate of altar calls, passing out tracks, and leading people to Christ. However, the prayer cannot come without a serious faith in the heart that Jesus is who He says that He is and that the person truly wants to be delivered from sin (John 3:16; Rom. 10:9, 10. 13).

What I am saying is that people need to know what God is really like before claiming to have led them into salvation. The gospel is meant "to give the light of the knowledge of the glory of God in the face of Jesus Christ." It is meant to tell people what God is really like – His love for them, His mercy, His desire to be a Father to them, His desire to spend eternity with them. Salvation and eternal life is leading people to know God intimately and not just knowing a bunch of intellectual gospel facts (John 17:3).

One of the reasons people are rejecting Christ is because He is so falsely represented. He is either misrepresented by the rabid atheists who hate Him, the buffoon comedians who make fun of Him, or, sadly, by the Christian theologians who add fuel to the fire by giving a false representation of Him under the guise of teaching "theology." These are distortions given by the blinding power of Satan. We must, by our words and example, show the truth to the world that Jesus is not the One who sends tragedy, sickness, and oppression. He is the Healer, the Deliverer, and Savior. This is why miracles must accompany our gospel preaching (Mark 16:15-20; Luke 10:1-9, 17-20; Matt. 10:1-8). Jesus said:

> *And this gospel of the kingdom shall be preached in all the world for a witness unto all nations; and then shall the end come* (Matt. 24:14)

When we have brought the gospel to the ends of the earth and everyone has had a chance to accept or reject Christ then the Lord will bring an end to the pain and misery that His people suffer. We are very close as so many missionaries are going to unreached territory and radio, television and internet has reached regions that may have been impossible to reach in times past. We should support these efforts through our finances and prayer.

Finally, for the cynics and scoffers that cry, "if God were a good God then He would get rid of evil." Oh, you should be glad that in His love and mercy He has not yet done it or you would be ridden of as well (John 3:18).

The Church Isn't Exactly Ready Yet

Another problem that God faces right now is that His very own bride is not exactly ready for Him to come back yet. Many of the "people of God" are still living in sin and worldliness. Jesus is very serious about the type of church that He is coming back for:

> *Husbands, love your wives, even as Christ also loved the church, and gave himself for it; That he might sanctify and cleanse it with the washing of water by the word, That he might present it to himself a glorious church, not having spot, or wrinkle, or any such thing; but that it should be holy and without blemish* (Eph. 5:25-27)

Many have been deceived by false messages of grace that tell us that once a person is in grace that they are always in grace. In other words, if one becomes a Christian but continues to sin, with no desire or intention to repent, they are told that God's blood still covers them and they remain in His grace and mercy.

There are a number of variations of this teaching, but for the insincere believer looking to continue the indulgences of the flesh, any variation of it suits their itching ears. What God's people do not understand is that sin puts blemishes upon God's people and it is the opposite of holiness. The writer of Hebrews (who I firmly believe is Paul) tells us that we will not see God apart from holiness:

> *Follow peace with all men, and **holiness, without which no man shall see the Lord**: Looking diligently **lest any man fail of the grace of God**; lest any root of bitterness springing up trouble you, and thereby many be defiled* (Heb. 12:14-15)

This is serious business. The apostle says here that a person can fail of God's grace. This "once in grace, always in grace" teaching simply is not in accordance with God's Word. Furthermore, one can become defiled. Sin has a tendency to defile the one sinning. But even more, the apostle says that apart from holiness *no man* shall see the Lord.

Many in the church today are steeped in sin, primarily sexual sin. Many men and women are "shacking up" and living together apart from holy matrimony. Many pastors have women on the side that are not their wives. Many of God's people are continually watching television programs and movies that promote worldly values and concepts. Even worse, many church-goers are addicted to pornography, alcohol, and drugs.

This is only touching the surface. Many ministers are compromising with the world and accepting so called "gay marriage" into the church. A number of pastors openly support politicians who advocate murdering innocent unborn children (abortion). Others are so involved in strife and war that no one can tell the difference between them and the world. Is this the church that Jesus is coming back for?

> *But fornication, and all uncleanness, or covetousness, let it not be once named among you, as becometh saints; Neither filthiness, nor foolish talking, nor jesting, which are not convenient: but rather giving of thanks. For this ye know, that no whoremonger, nor unclean person, nor covetous man, who is an idolater,* **hath any inheritance in the kingdom of Christ and of God** (Eph. 5:3-5)

While we are crying about Christ taking so long to return, Christ's delay is actually an act of God's **mercy**, not only for those who have never heard the truth about Christ, but even for His very own church who have not yet learned to walk holy. He is coming back for a church without spot or wrinkle.

We want Him to come back soon, but we must take seriously the admonition of our Lord: *"Therefore be ye also ready: for in such an hour as ye think not the Son of man cometh"* (Matt. 24:44). When the church has put away evil within it then we will be ready for Christ to come and rid the world of it.

Notes

Chapter One
1. Bertoluci, Jose M. **The Son of the Morning and the Guardian Cherub in the Context of the Controversy Between Good and Evil** (Th.D. dissertation, Andrews University Seventh-day Adventist Theological Seminary, 1985. Available from University Microfilms, University of Michigan, P.O. Box 1346, Ann Arbor, MI 48106-1346)., p. 593
2. Larkin, Clarence **The Spirit World** (Mansfield Centre, CT: Martino Publishing, 2011), p. 14
3. Pember, G. H. **Earth's Earliest Ages** (Grand Rapids, MI: Kregel Publications, 1876, 1975), p. 51
4. See again Bertoluci, *The Son of the Morning*. I recommend this dissertation only for the one who is interested in the most thorough research I have seen to date concerning the history of interpretation in which Isa. 14 and Ezek. 28 are seen as references to Satan and how only within Reformed and modern day scholarship has this interpretation been disputed.
5. "Tertullian against Marcion" as cited in Roberts, Reverend Alexander **The Ante-Nicene Fathers: Volume III** (New York: Cosimo, Inc. 2007), p. 305
6. Derek Prince offers us an insightful commentary here: "Scripture confronts us with a deliberate contrast between Lucifer and Jesus. Lucifer was not in the form of God; he was a created being. He had no right to be equal with God. Yet he grasped at equality with God, and when he reached up, he slipped and fell. On the other hand, Jesus was divine by eternal nature and enjoyed equality with God. He did not need to grasp at it, but rather, He humbled Himself." Prince, Derek **War in Heaven: God's Epic Battle with Evil** (Grand Rapids, MI: Chosen Books, 2003), p. 63

Chapter Four
1. Pember, *Earth's Earliest Ages*, p.52
2. Lindsay, Gordon **Satan's Rebellion and Fall** (Dallas, TX: Christ for the Nations, 1981), pp. 10-11
3. Ibid, p. 7
4. Kalinowski, Mark **Why God didn't Kill the Devil** (Life Tabernacle Church, 2005), P. 58
5. Luginbill, Robert D. **The Satanic Rebellion: Background to the Tribulation Part 1**, http://ichthys.com (Last accessed: May 31, 2011)

6. Marston, Paul and Forster, Roger **God's Strategy in Human History** (Eugen, Oregon, Wipf and Stock Publishers, 2000), p. 7
7. Lindsay, *Satan's Rebellion*, p. 7
8. Bounds, E. M. **Guide to Spiritual Warfare** (New Kinsington, PA: Whitaker House, 1984), p. 33

Chapter Five
1. Luginbill, *The Satanic Rebellion*, http://ichthys.com (Last accessed: May 31, 2011)
2. Epp, Theodore H. **Practical Studies in Revelation (Vol. II)** (Lincoln, NE: Back to the Bible, 1969), p. 362
3. Simpson, Albert B. **The Christ in the Bible Commentary, Volume 6** (Camp Hill, PA: Christian Publications, 1994), p. 512

Chapter Six
1. Murray, John Hale **A Help for English Readers to Understand Mis-translated Passages in Our Bible** (London: S. W. Partridge & Co., 1881), p. 2
2. Ibid, pp. 144, 145
3. Alexander, Victor **Book of Isaiah: Translated from the Aramaic Scriptures** (Kindle Edition) (Burbank, CA: Victor Alexander, 2012)
4. Ibid.
5. Kaiser Jr., Walter C. **Hard Sayings of the Bible** (Downers Grove, IL: Intervarsity Press, 1996), p. 306
6. Thornton, R. & Billings, J **Expounder of Primitive Christianity Volume 2** (Philadelphia, 1846), p. 346

Chapter Seven
1. Matson, William A. **The Adversary, His Person, Power, and Purpose: A Study in Satanology** (New York: E.S. Gorham, 1902), p. 61
2. Jamieson-Fausset-Brown Bible Commentary, http://biblehub.com/isaiah/40-22.htm (Last accessed: March 23, 2015)
3. Clark, Douglas R.; Brunt, John C. (editors) **Introducing the Bible Volume I: The Old Testament and Intertestamental Literature** (New York: University Press of America, 1997), p. 171
4. Schauffler, Adolphus Frederick **Select Notes on the International Sunday School Lessons** (W. A. Wilde Company, 1875), pp. 25-26
5. Scott, Walter **The Existence of Evil Spirits Proved: and their Agency, Particularly in Relation to the Human Race, Explained and Illustrated** (Jackson and Walford, 1843), pp. 94, 95

6. Cowles, Henry **Hebrew History from the Death of Moses to the Close of the Scripture Narrative** (New York: D. Appleton & Co., 1875), p. 207

Chapter Eight
1. Plues, Robert **The Peculiarities of Calvinism Tested** (London: G. J. Stevenson, 1862), p. 62
2. Calvin, John **Institutes of the Christian Religion**, Book 3, Chapter 23, section 8
3. Palmer, Edwin **The Five Points of Calvinism**, 1999
4. Dake, Finis J. **God's Plan For Man** (Lawrenceville, GA: Dake's Bible Sales, 1949, 1977), p. 621
5. Vine's Complete Expository Dictionary of Old and New Testament Words: With Topical Index (Thomas Nelson Inc, 1996)
6. Olson, Gordon C. **The Foreknowledge of God: An Inquiry as to the Truthfulness of the Doctrine, Theologically and Scripturally** (Arlington Heights, Il: The Bible Research Corporation, 1941), p. 17

Chapter Eleven
1. It is true that if one rejects Christ then God's wrath abides on him (John 3:36) but we must have a Biblical understanding of the wrath of God that is consistent with His love. Paul tells us in Romans 1 that God's wrath has been revealed and then goes on to explain exactly what *the wrath of God* is. He tells us that God's wrath is the forsaking of the sinner to the consequences of his or her sin (Rom. 1:26-28). This is consistent with many other passages of Scripture that speak about God's wrath or His anger (Deut. 31:17-18; 1 Kings 14:15-16; 2 Kings 17:17-20; 2 Chron. 29:6-8; Isa. 57:17; Jer. 33:5). It is our *sin* that separates us from God, removing us from under the umbrella of His protection and leaving us at the mercy of sin's consequences (Isa. 59:1-2; Eph. 2:1-5).This is the "wrath of God". Jesus experienced this wrath for us (Matt. 27:46) so that we don't have to.
2. Vine's Expository Dictionary of Biblical Words
3. Strong, James. **The New Strong's Exhaustive Concordance of the Bible**, Copyright (C) 1984 by Thomas Nelson Publishers.
4. Murray, Andrew **With Christ in the School of Prayer** (Springdale, PA: Whitaker House, 1981), p. 133

Chapter Twelve
1. Vincent, Marvin, Vincent's Word Studies (Online version available at http://www.godrules.net)
2. Robertson, A.T. Robertson's Word Pictures In The New Testament (Online version available at http://www.godrules.net)

3. Gordon, Samuel D. **Quiet Talks on Personal Problems** (New York: Eaton and Mains, 1907), pp. 28-29

Chapter Thirteen
1. Pink, Arthur W. **The Sovereignty of God** (Pensacola, FL: Chapel Library, 1993), on page 74 Pink is offering a rebuttal to an unnamed book on prayer (which I personally think is a book written by one of my favorites, E. M. Bounds). The book correctly speaks about how prayer changes destinies. Because this goes against Pink's false teaching about an all-controlling deity he writes in response, "To say that 'human destiny' may be changed by the will of man is to make the creature's will supreme, and that is, virtually, to dethrone God. But what saith the Scriptures? Let the Book answer" to which he cites Hannah's prayer in 1 Sam. 2:6-8. As we will see, Pink and others who use this passage incorrectly failed to interpret Scripture in light of other Scripture that explains God's actions in light of the permissive idiom prevalent in the culture during Hannah's time.
2. Dodd, C. H. **The Epistle of Paul to the Romans** (New York: Harper and Brothers Publishers,), pp. 137, 138
3. Ferguson, Fergus **The Character of God** (General Books Publication, 2009), p. 21

Chapter Fourteen
1. Hobbs, Herschel H. **The Cosmic Drama: An Exposition of the Book of Revelation** (Waco, TX: Word Book Publishers, 1971), p. 194
2. Simpson, *Christ in the Bible*, pp. 522, 523

Other books from
Vindicating God Ministries!

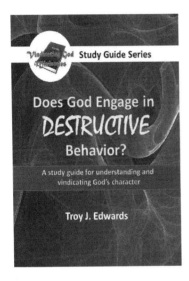

Does God Engage in DESTRUCTIVE Behavior?
A study guide for understanding and vindicating God's character

What we believe about God will affect our lives. It will determine how we raise our children, treat our spouses, deal with strangers, interact with fellow employees, and how we conduct our ministry to the Lord and others. After this study you will love God and your Bible even more

How?
A look at God's character in light of Biblical passages that are inconsistent with love

This book looks at a number of God's acts recorded in the Bible that paint Him as malicious, harsh, hypocritical, and in some cases, worse than the humans whose sin He punishes. The explanations that the Bible offers will help you see God in a new light. The reader will discover that God has always explained the punitive language of Scripture within the Bible.

Visit www.vindicatinggod.org

Other books from
Vindicating God Ministries!

Does God Send Sickness?
Vindicating God's character concerning sickness and disease
God has been taking the blame for sickness and disease for centuries. This book will look at some difficult Bible passages in light of the *permissive idiom of the ancient Hebrew language,* in which God is often said to do the things that He merely allowed or permitted to happen.

Does God Send Natural Disasters?
Vindicating God's character concerning Accidents and Disasters
Some call natural disasters "acts of God". However, does the Bible actually teach that God is the One sending them? Using the "permission idiom" we will examine several Bible disasters and learn that Scripture teaches us that God is actually trying to protect the world from disasters.

Visit www.vindicatinggod.org

Other books from
Vindicating God Ministries!

Stop Blaming God
For the Work of the Enemy
This book shows from Scripture that God is not the source of any of our problems. It deals with a number of areas in which God is blamed and helps you to see that God is not at fault for the problems in life and that we can have the victory in every situation if we focus on exactly who our enemy is.

God is Said to do that which He Only Permits
Exploring a Neglected Principle of Bible Interpretation that Vindicates God's Character
This book explores "the permission idiom" in which God is said to be the cause of that which He merely allowed or did not prevent. Neglect of this idiom has led to much misunderstanding about God and the Bible. This book will help you that there is no darkness in God (1 John 1:5).

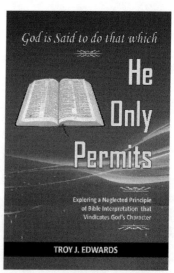

Visit www.vindicatinggod.org

Also coming soon from
Vindicating God Ministries!

Vindicating God
A unique daily devotional that defends God against false accusations made against Him

There are sincere worshippers of Christ who love Him dearly but are quite ignorant of how to deal with difficult passages in the Bible that might be used by God's enemies to paint a false picture of Him. These daily devotions give a better understanding about God's character.

Untying God's "NOTS!"
Or, How Much Control Does God Really Have?

Many Christians love to use the phrase, "God is in Control." Some take it to mean that all circumstances, good and evil, come from God. Others take it to mean that God is sovereign and omnipotent and will work in your situation if you let Him. This book examines the "God is in Control" idea in light of Scripture.

Visit www.vindicatinggod.org

Made in the USA
Middletown, DE
26 October 2023

41222566R00102